Take Another Letter

Geoffrey M. Myers

PHOENIX
ELT
incorporating
PRENTICE HALL MACMILLAN

New York London Toronto Sydney Tokyo Singapore

Published 1996 by
Phoenix ELT
Campus 400, Spring Way
Maylands Avenue, Hemel Hempstead
Hertfordshire, HP2 7EZ
A division of Prentice Hall International

First published 1987 by Macmillan Publishers Ltd

Printed and bound in Malaysia

A CIP catalogue record for this book is available from the British Library

ISBN 0 13 435561 X

9 8 7 6 5
99 98 97 96

ACKNOWLEDGEMENTS

With a few obvious exceptions, the companies and individuals featured in this book are fictitious.
The telephone, telex and box numbers are fictitious in their relationship to the addresses.

Contents

Introduction

This book has been designed as a follow-up to ***Take a Letter*** but it can also be used by intermediate students who have no previous knowledge of business correspondence. The first unit quickly revises the layout of the letter while the rest of the book concentrates on the language of letter-writing itself, with special emphasis laid on the build up of vocabulary.

A new feature is the 'Back up task' at the end of most units. This gives students adequate opportunity for further practice. However, because sometimes several letters are involved in this exercise, considerations of space have made it impossible to include blank pages for this.

Another novelty is the use of recorded material, including a dictation given in an office setting for every chapter.

Many different styles of layout and punctuation are used in letter-writing, of course. The system followed here is called 'open punctuation'. It employs no punctuation in the basic layout, and is common office practice today. Some of the printed letterheads show accepted variations.

Standard business terminology, including one or two insurance/legal terms, and abbreviations used in the book are defined in the appendix. Although ***Take Another Letter*** is 'set' in the 1980s, the precise year has usually been left blank. Students must fill this in where appropriate.

Unit 1

Laying out the letter

1 Mr Hernando Garcia is the manager of a large toy shop in Spain. He has just been to the famous Toy Fair in Nuremburg (West Germany) and has ordered twenty fluffy koalas and twenty fluffy kangaroos. When he returns home he receives this letter.

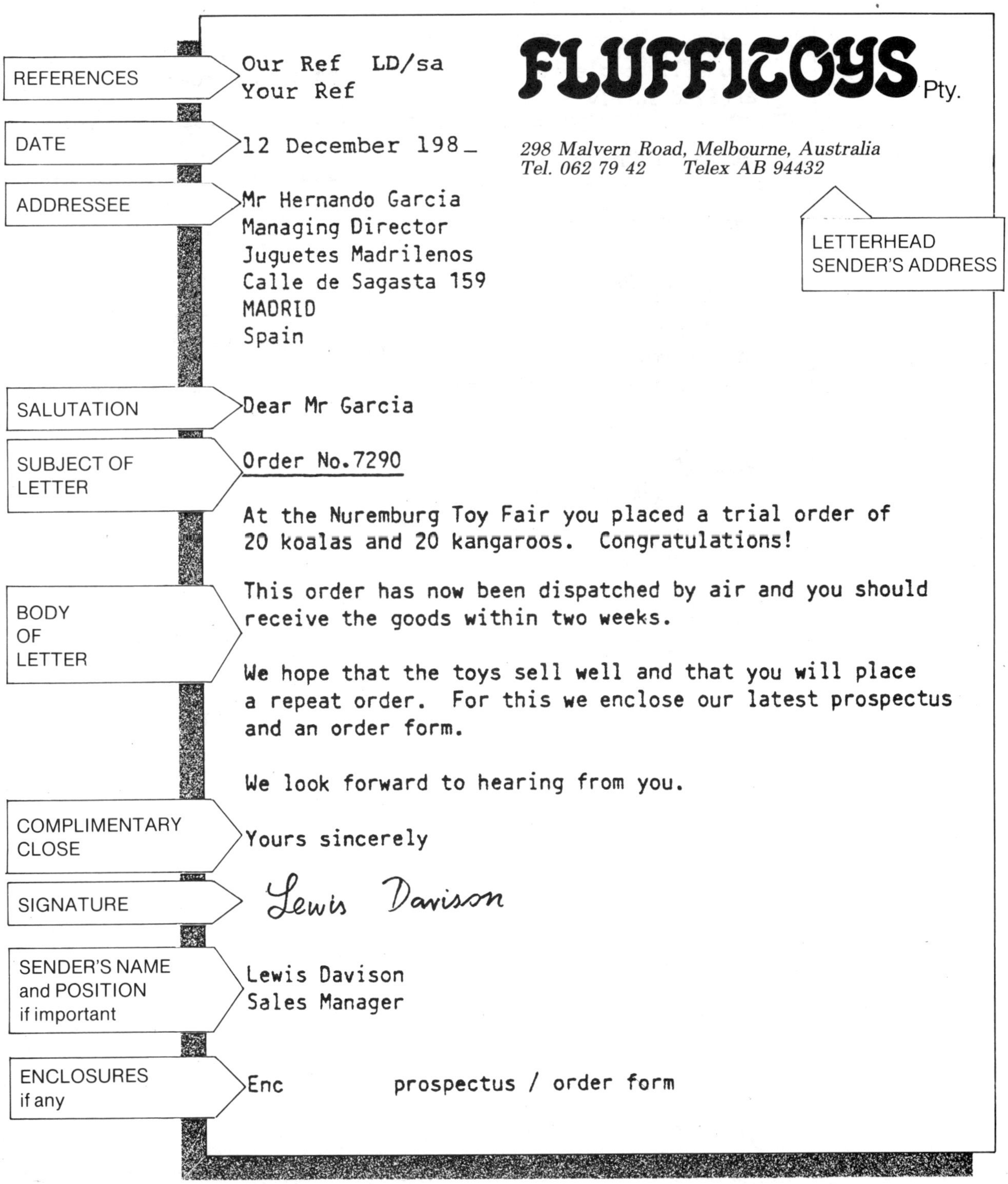

Our Ref LD/sa
Your Ref

FLUFFITOYS Pty.

298 Malvern Road, Melbourne, Australia
Tel. 062 79 42 Telex AB 94432

12 December 198_

Mr Hernando Garcia
Managing Director
Juguetes Madrilenos
Calle de Sagasta 159
MADRID
Spain

Dear Mr Garcia

Order No.7290

At the Nuremburg Toy Fair you placed a trial order of 20 koalas and 20 kangaroos. Congratulations!

This order has now been dispatched by air and you should receive the goods within two weeks.

We hope that the toys sell well and that you will place a repeat order. For this we enclose our latest prospectus and an order form.

We look forward to hearing from you.

Yours sincerely

Lewis Davison

Lewis Davison
Sales Manager

Enc prospectus / order form

2 The fluffy koalas and kangaroos are so successful that Mr Garcia decides to place a repeat order. He writes to Fluffitoys, but unfortunately the letter falls into the office shredder by mistake.

Look at the letter on p. 1 and use that to help you put this letter in the right order.

Then fill in the 'parts of the letter'.

18 January 198_

Dear Mr Davison

Yours sincerely

You will be pleased to hear that the above order
arrived safely.

Hernando Garcia

Enc order form

<u>Order No.7290</u>

Our customers were delighted and all the toys were
sold out within two weeks.

Juguetes
Madrilenos S.A.

Mr L. Davison
Sales Manager

Calle de Sagasta 159 Madrid Spain tel 01 290 333

Our ref HG / cs
Your ref LD / sa

Managing Director

Fluffitoys Pty
298 Malvern Road

We are therefore placing a repeat order for 100 of
each, and look forward to receiving the goods.

Melbourne
Australia

H Garcia

Parts of the letter

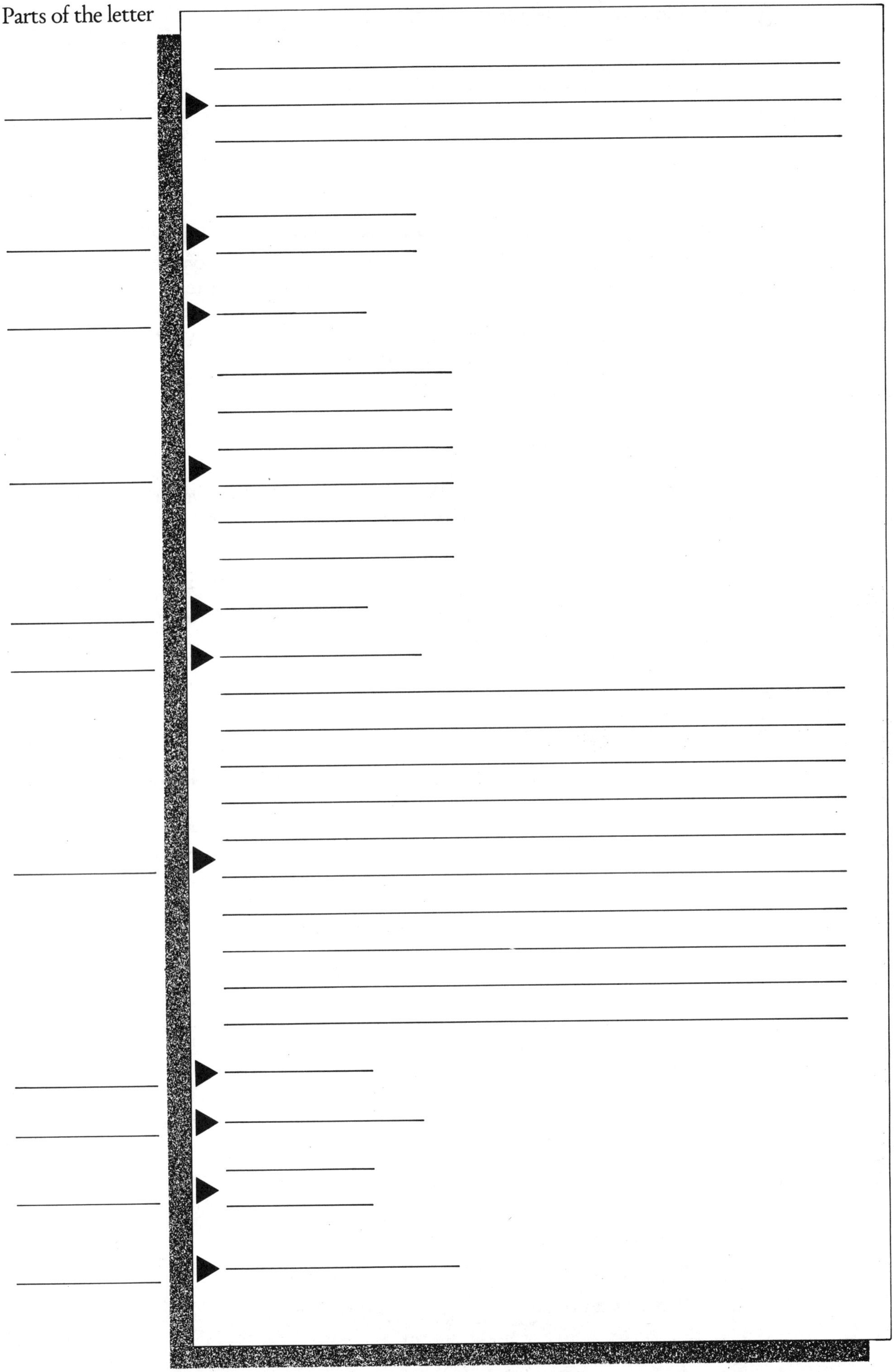

3 Let us look more closely at some of the parts of the letter.

A The *references*
Look at the letter on p. 1 again. You will see:

Your ref
Our ref

This means *your reference* and *our reference*. A reference is useful for filing. It tells you who wrote and signed the letter (the boss) and then who typed it (the secretary). A reference may also include a file number and a date.
Our ref LD/sa in that letter means that *L*ewis *D*avison wrote it and his secretary, *S*arah *A*spinal, typed it. LD and SA are their *initials*. What are your initials? When you reply to a business letter, you fill in that letter's reference as 'Your ref' and add your own as 'Our ref'.

Now fill in 'Our ref' below.

Ahmed Karim wrote it Fawzia Sadiq typed it		John Pratt wrote it You typed it		You wrote it Janet Lee typed it	
Your ref	JB/rl	Your ref	HOL/87	Your ref	MED/6/cb
Our ref	_____	Our ref	_____	Our ref	_____

B The *salutation* and the *complimentary close*

	If we **know** the name of the addressee, we begin:	If we **do not know** the name of the addressee, we begin:
Salutation ▶	Dear Mr Smith Dear Miss Hill	Dear Sir (to a man) Dear Madam (to a woman)
	and we end:	and we end:
Complimentary close ▶	Yours sincerely	Yours faithfully

If we are writing to a company or department and do not know exactly who to write to, we write 'Dear Sirs', as in the examples.

```
Dixit Computers
Rubensplein 24
Haarlem
The Netherlands

Dear Sirs
```

```
The British Tourist Authority
Thames Tower
Black's Road
London W6

Dear Sirs
```

Now fill in the salutation and complimentary close for these people.

1 The Chairman
Asta Products Inc.
100 West 23 Street
New York NY 10010
U S A

Dear ____________

Yours ____________

2 Mrs G. Faella
24 via Farnese
Rome
Italy

Dear ____________

Yours ____________

3 The Tourist Office
Ataturk Caddesi
Izmir
Turkey

Dear ____________

Yours ____________

4 The Manageress
Modern Fashions
Kallang Road
Singapore

Dear ____________

Yours ____________

5 Japinvest Corp.
3-3-4 Otsuka
Bunkyo-ku
Tokyo 112

Dear ____________

Yours ____________

6 Mr Ben Mzima
Coral Beach Hotel
Mombasa
Kenya

Dear ____________

Yours ____________

C *Subject of the letter*

Sometimes we write a heading at the top of the letter. It is called the *subject of the letter*. It tells us exactly what the letter is about, for example, the number of an order or invoice.

It is placed after the salutation and it is usually underlined or written in BLOCK LETTERS.

Dear Mr Hassan

Order No. B-270

We have received the above order

Sometimes the word 'Re' is used. This means 'about', 'concerning'.

Dear Miss Lee

Re: Your Insurance Policy No. 120.4967

D *Enclosures*
If you put something in with your letter, like a cheque or a prospectus, you are enclosing something. Then you write 'Enc', short for *enclosure*, at the bottom of the letter, with or without the object you are enclosing.

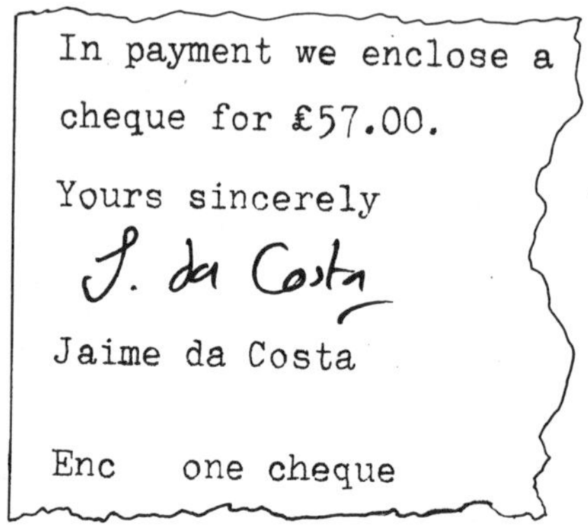
In payment we enclose a cheque for £57.00.

Yours sincerely

J. da Costa

Jaime da Costa

Enc one cheque

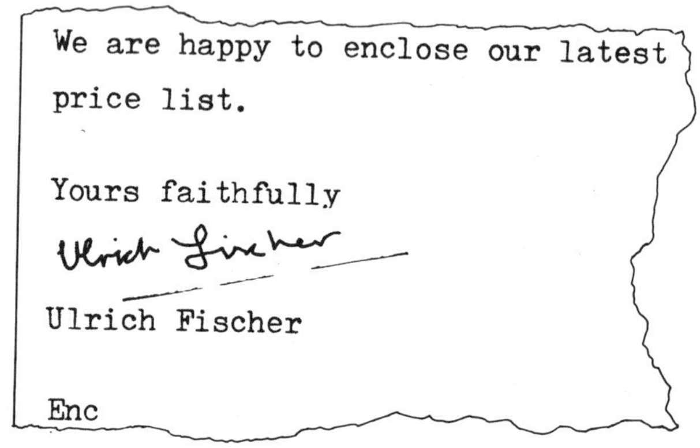
We are happy to enclose our latest price list.

Yours faithfully

Ulrich Fischer

Ulrich Fischer

Enc

4 QUIZ

Do you know these words?

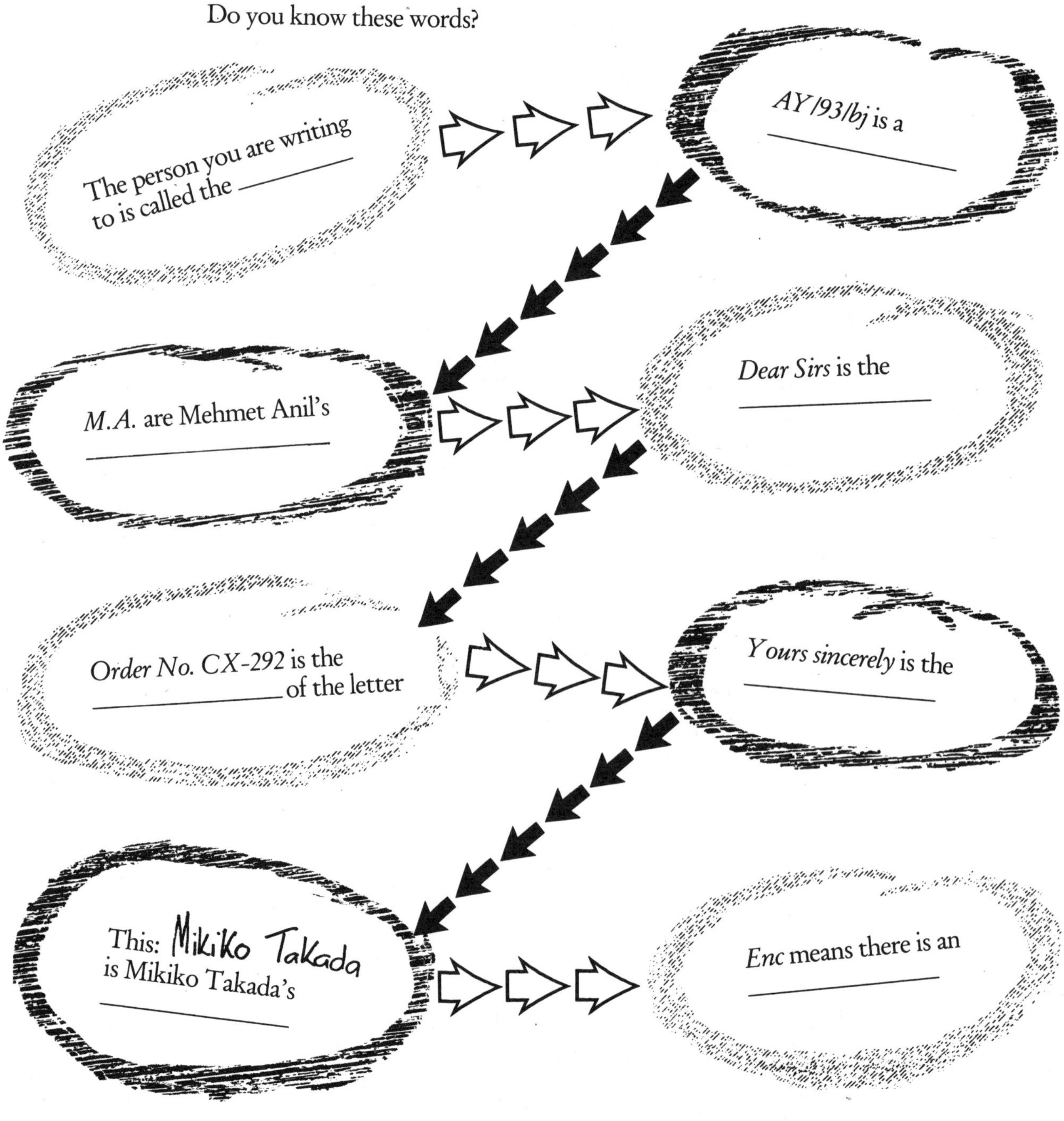

5 Dictation

Fill in the missing words in this letter.

Dear ________

________________ No. ________

When you ________ ____ ______ Basle Watch Fair in Switzerland ______ ______ you placed a ______ ______ ____ ____ of our watches.

We are ______ __ ______ ____ that this ________ ____ ____ ____ ____________ by air and you should __________ ___ ________ ___ ________.

We are sure ______ ____ ______ will sell well and that you will ________ ____ ________ ________ soon.

We ________ ____ ________ showing all our ________ models, and ________ ________ ____ ________ ______ ______.

________ ________

6 Vocabulary exercise

All these words are in Unit 1. What are they? The first and last letters are given.

very happy, very pleased	d - - ◯ - - - - d
part of a company	d - - - - - - - ◯ t
doing very well	s - - - - ◯ - - ◯ l
you are sorry to say, but . . .	u - - - ◯ - - - ◯ - - - y
a bill, something you pay	i ◯ - - - ◯ e
the subject of the letter is often	u - - - - - - - ◯ d

All the letters in the circles spell a word meaning: money you pay in case something is stolen, or you have an accident.

An - - - - - - - - - policy.

Unit 2
Asking for information

1 **Question** *What do all these people want?*

My sixty room hotel is being renovated at the moment. What I need is a much more modern telephone switchboard. I must get some quotations.

Mr Kemal Turan
Hotel owner, Turkey

I saw some of the latest equipment at a trade fair recently. We need machines like that in our factory. But I'll need some more details first.

Mr Y. Matsumotu
Manager of textile factory, Japan

I want to learn English in England this year. I've got some addresses from the British Council. Now I'll have to write for some prospectuses.

Miss Ana Ferreira
Student, Portugal

New cutlery. Knives, forks, spoons, 200 of each of them, large and small. That's what I need. Look at these old things. Can't eat with those.

Mr Jorge Soler
has just bought a restaurant, Argentina

What I need right now is a holiday, I can tell you! Somewhere quiet and sunny. How about a flat in Ibiza? Here's an interesting advertisement. I'll write off today.

Mrs Ethel James
Clothes shop manageress, UK

Answer Further information

2 Building up the letter

Asking for information. We also say *requesting* information.

A business letter is usually in three parts.

A The beginning This says how you heard about the addressee.

We have seen your advertisement in	Far East Business. The Financial Times. In Britain. (your local paper) ________________

or:

I met your representative We saw your equipment cutlery	when he visited Egypt at Expo Japan at the Hanover Trade Fair	this year. in June. last spring.

or:

I have got your address from I have heard about you from You were recommended to me by	my teacher, Mr/Mrs/Miss ____________ a business friend, Mr Paul Wilkins. the British Council. the British Tourist Authority.

Write four sentences like this.

____

____

____

____

____

____

____

____

____

____

B The middle In this part you often give the exact reason why you are looking for further information.

Look at these sentences and write similar ones using the words given.

a We have recently bought a restaurant and would like to replace the cutlery.
We / moved into new offices / install new equipment.

____

____

We / expanded our business / stock a wider range of products.

____

____

b We are now replacing our old machines and are interested in newer models.
We / expanding our premises / a modern shelving system.

____

____

We / renovating our store / a new air-conditioning system.

____

____

c My hotel is being renovated and I am looking for new bedroom furniture.
Our offices / redecorated / new fitted carpets.

____

____

Our stock / expanded / new lines of stationery.

____

____

d

I intend I have decided I hope	to come to England for three months to spend my holidays in Spain to visit your town to rent a flat in London	this summer. this year. next spring. in July.

Write two sentences like this.

____

____

____

____

e Next comes the request.

We would be grateful if you could Please	send us me	further more	details. information.
		your latest brochure. your catalogue. lists of flats. addresses of hotels.	

Write two sentences like this.

____

____

____

____

C **The end.** This is what we often say at the end of a letter like this.

We look forward to hearing I hope to hear	from you	soon. in the near future.

Write two sentences like this.

____

____

3 Writing the letter

Look at p. 8 again and write one letter for one of the men and one for one of the women. Use the 'building up the letter' section to help you, and try to use different sentences in each letter. Begin 'Dear Sirs'.

4 Replying to a request for information

Building up the letter

A The beginning

We acknowledge receipt of Thank you for We have received	your inquiry your letter	of 2 March. of 15 June. of 31 August.

Write two sentences like this.

B The middle You give the information required, or enclose the prospectus requested.

<table>
<tr><td>We are pleased to enclose
send you</td><td rowspan="2">our latest</td><td rowspan="2">catalogue.
prospectus.
leaflet.
price list.</td></tr>
<tr><td>We have pleasure in enclosing
sending you</td></tr>
</table>

Write two sentences like this.

C The end You should always be ready to give the customer further information if he requires it.

<table>
<tr><td rowspan="2">If you</td><td colspan="2">require further information</td><td rowspan="2">please do not hesitate to</td><td rowspan="2">contact us.
write to us.</td></tr>
<tr><td>have any</td><td>special requests
other questions</td></tr>
</table>

NOTE: If we write this sentence, we do not have to end with 'We are looking forward to your reply'.

Write two sentences like this.

5 Writing the letter

Now write a reply to one of your letters on p. 8.

6 Dictation

New instruction:
Cross out = Put a line through.

7 Active and Passive

We use the passive a lot in letter-writing, especially when the thing we do is more important than who does it.

A We are doing something now. PRESENT CONTINUOUS

Example: ACTIVE We are renovating our hotel.
PASSIVE Our hotel *is being renovated.*

Passive is formed with *is/are* + *being* + past participle.

Now you do it.

1 We are replacing our old typewriters.

____

2 We are redecorating our office.

____

3 We are expanding our premises.

____

4 We are installing a new switchboard.

____

5 We are stocking a wider range.

____

B We have just done something. PRESENT PERFECT

Example: ACTIVE We have just/recently redecorated our offices.
PASSIVE Our offices *have* just/recently *been redecorated.*

Passive is formed with *has/have* + *been* + past participle.

Now you do it.

1 We have recently renovated our staff canteen.

____

2 We have just replaced all our cutlery.

____

3 We have recently installed a new shelving system.

____

4 We have just expanded our range of products.

____

5 We have recently rebuilt our warehouses.

____

8 Vocabulary exercise

Replace the words in *italics* with others from this unit which mean the same.

Example: We are *making* our department *bigger*.
We are **expanding** our department.

1 If you *want more* information, do not *wait* to contact us.

____

2 We are going to buy new *knives, forks and spoons*. (= one word)

____

3 Typewriters, telex machines, calculators are all office *machines*.

____

4 I'll have to write off for some *prospectuses*.

____

5 Mr Turan wants a company to *put in* a new switchboard.

____

6 Do you stock *paper, pens, pencils and rubbers*? (= one word)

____

7 We want to sell *new lines* of goods.

We want to sell a wider ______ of goods.

9 Vocabulary exercise

In this unit there are a lot of words beginning with *re-*. Do you know them all? Example: an answer *reply*.

1	to ask for	. . . .
2	to need	. . . .
3	to get (a letter in the post)	. . . .
4	to throw away old things and get new ones	. . . .
5	a short time ago	. . . .
6	to make a building new	. . . .
7	to tell something good about something	. . . .
8	a place where you go to eat	. . . .
9	to paint a room again	. . . .
10	a person who *represents* a company	. . . .

Little words out of big words

REPRESENTATIVE. How many smaller words can you find in this word? You can use each letter once only in your word. Examples: AT, EAT, IT, SIT.

If you find 10 words, good. 20 words, very good. 30 words, excellent.

Back up task

Mr Spiros Petrides, of the Cyprus Agricultural Development Board, intends to visit England from 10–16 November, and he wants to hire a car (middle category).

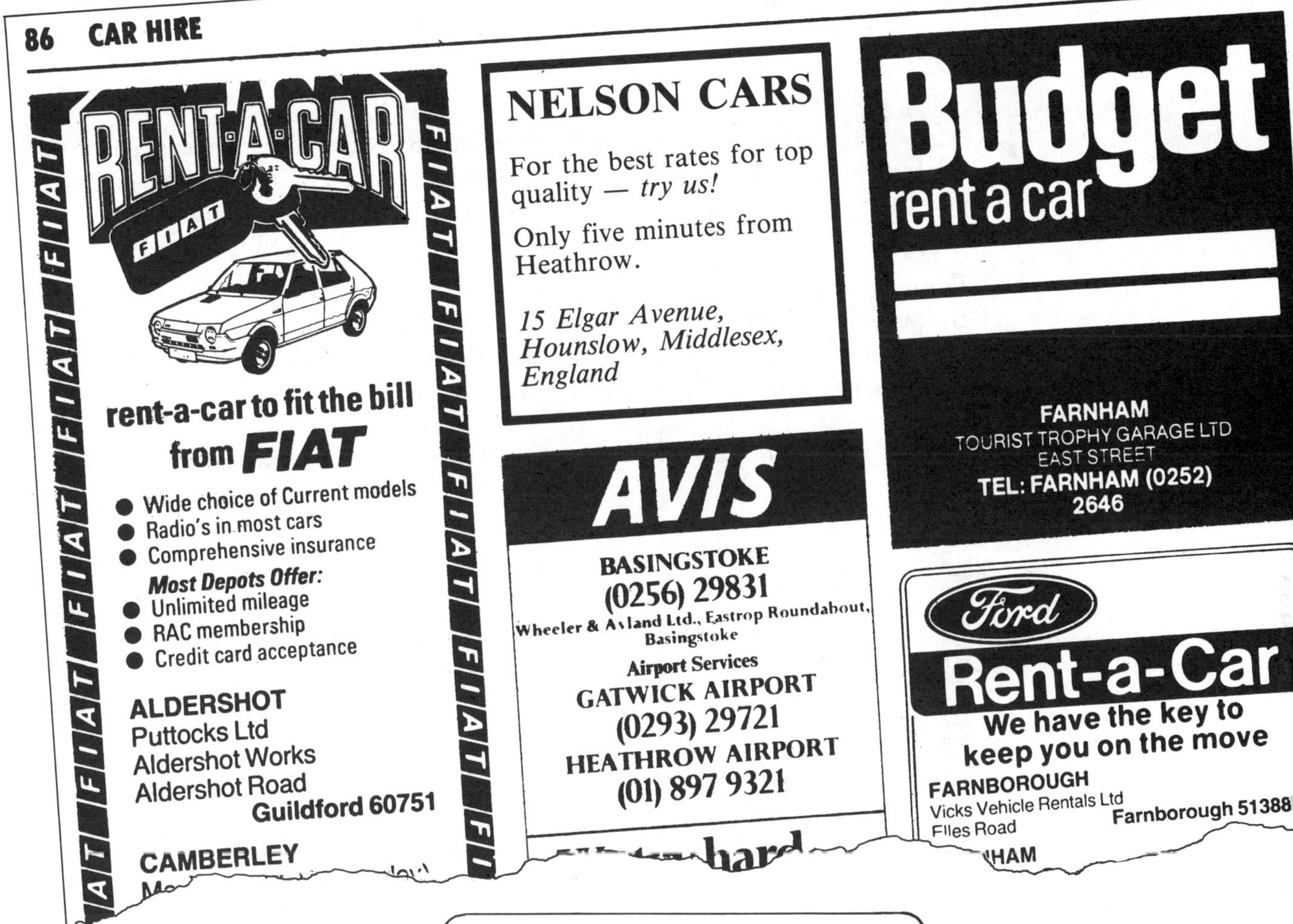

Unit 3

Receiving a quotation

1 After you have looked through prospectuses, catalogues and price lists, you usually ask for a detailed quotation for the goods you require. This includes the cost of the goods, any discounts, the cost and method of freight, insurance and the terms of payment.

For most large international orders today prices are quoted CIF, which means that the price includes the Cost, Insurance and Freight to a port or airport of destination which the customer indicates. Payment is usually made by L/C (Letter of Credit) which you arrange through your bank.

Look at these examples. The first is one of the quotations received by Mr Jorge Soler.

Dear Mr Soler

Thank you for the interest you have shown in our products.

We are very happy to submit a quotation CIF Buenos Aires for the cutlery you require.

Large dinner knives "Victoria"	200	at	£2 each	£400
Large dinner forks	"		£2	£400
Large soup spoons	"		£2	£400
Dessert knives	"		£1.50	£300
Dessert forks	"		£1.50	£300
Dessert spoons	"		£1.50	£300
Fish knives	"		£1.80	£360
Fish forks	"		£1.80	£360
				£2520
	less discount at 15%			378
				£2142
			packing	£75
			freight	£280
			insurance	£70
				£2567

As you can see, we are prepared to grant a 15% discount on this order. The transport quoted is airfreight and you should receive the goods within one week of our receipt of your order. Payment, in sterling, should be made by Letter of Credit.

We look forward to receiving your firm order.

Yours sincerely

J. H. Walker

p.p. Harris & Williams
Master cutlers

2 A quotation is normally for the supply of goods. When we make inquiries about a service we often use the word *estimate*. An estimate is an exact idea of the cost of a job which has to be done, for example, repainting the outside of a hotel, redecorating offices, installing a new machine. A very detailed estimate is usually submitted on a separate sheet.

This is one of the replies Mr Kemal Turan received.

Dear Mr Turan

Further to your inquiry about our telephone switchboards, we would recommend for a hotel of your size (60 rooms) the PABX C-50 model, which is computerised and fully automatic. You will see further details about this very popular model in the enclosed brochure.

We are pleased to submit the following quotation:

PABX C-50	£15,600
Packing, Insurance and Freight (Road) to Istanbul	£ 1,600
Total cost of installation	£ 1,850
Grand total	£19,050

A team of two of our installation engineers would fly to Istanbul to install the C-50. Estimated installation time, three days. The work could be completed within six days of the receipt of your firm order. Please refer to the enclosed estimate for full details.

If you are able to accommodate our engineers in your hotel during their stay, we are prepared to offer a discount of £200.

Payment, in sterling, to be arranged through your bank, one third with order, the balance on completion.

We hope you will find this offer acceptable and look forward to hearing from you.

Yours sincerely

And this is the one Mr Petrides received.

Dear Mr Petrides

Further to your letter of 10 September, we have pleasure in enclosing our latest prospectus. Please fill in the booking form and return it to us as soon as possible.

Our quotation for a seven day hire of a middle category (Group D) car, unlimited mileage, including full insurance, CDW, AA/RAC membership and VAT is:

Hire of car	£96
CDW	£12
	£108
VAT at 15%	16.20
Total	£124.20

Please note that the cost of petrol is not included in these rates.

If you have any further questions do not hesitate to contact us.

Yours sincerely

3 Joining sentences with 'Further to'. This means 'about'.
We sometimes join the first and second sentences like this.

> We have received your letter. We have pleasure in enclosing . . . .
> Further to your letter, we have pleasure in enclosing . . . .

Now you do it.

Thank you for your inquiry. We are happy to send you a catalogue . . .

____

I refer to our telephone conversation yesterday. We are pleased to confirm . . .

____

____

Write the reply from the other car hire company (for the same type of car). Use the table below for their prices. Remember, Mr Petrides is going in November. Look at p. 17 to help you.

1987 SELF-DRIVE RENTAL TARIFF

Rates are for UNLIMITED MILEAGE

Rates subject to change

GROUP	MODELS	DAILY RATE	WEEKLY RATE		
			Jun-Sep	Oct-Mar	Apr-May
		£	£	£	£
A	Fiesta 950	16	80	65	70
B	Fiesta 1100	18	85	70	75
C	Escort 1300	20	95	80	85
D	Escort 1600 Sierra 1600	24	110	100	105
E	Sierra 2.0 GL	28	120	110	115
Luxury cars: Mercedes, Jaguar, Porsche, Rolls-Royce. Prices on request.					

- COLLISION DAMAGE WAIVER (CDW)
  Groups A, B, C. £1.50 per day.
  Groups D, E. £2.00 per day.
  Minimum charge for CDW as for one week.
- INSURANCE
  Unlimited cover is provided against third party injuries and third party property damage.
  You are NOT covered for the first £200 of accidental damage to the hired car. If the COLLISION DAMAGE WAIVER is taken the driver is covered for ALL damage to the car.
- VAT (VALUE ADDED TAX — Government Tax) at 15% is not included in above rates.
- PETROL is not included.
- PRICES include free delivery Heathrow Airport on hires longer than one week.
- DELIVERY & COLLECTION SERVICES to/from other UK cities available at extra cost.

4 Listen to this conversation. Fill in the answers to the tourist's questions and the booking form.

The scene: at the garage of North London Car Hire.

NORTH LONDON CAR HIRE
Reservation form

Personal details

Name and initials of hirer ______________________

____

Occupation ______________________

Permanent home address ______________________

____

UK address and tel. no. ______________________

____

Drivers Licence no. ______________________

____

Expiry date ______________________

Payment — state type of credit card

____

Insurance details

Date of birth ______________________

Driving experience ________yrs

(A) Convictions in past 5 yrs ________

(B) Accidents in past 3 yrs ________

(C) Physical disabilities ________

If the answer to any question is 'yes', please inform us of the full details separately.

Vehicle details

Model required ______________________

____

From ____________ on ____________

To ____________ on ____________

I will collect the car from (*delete as necessary)

garage/Heathrow/Gatwick*

I will return the car to

garage/Heathrow/Gatwick*

Extras required

Roof rack ______________________

Child seat ______________________

Continental/Ireland touring ____________

Ferry bookings ______________________

Signed ______________________

Date ______________________

5 Mr Petrides decides to accept the Nelson offer.
Here are the details of his business trip to England and some of the documents he will take with him.

Use these to fill in his reservation form on the next page.

Cyprus Agricultural Development Board

Form C/14 Staff Overseas Itinerary

Name ____________________

Post __________ Department __________

Country visited ____________________

Date of departure ____________________

Flight no. (if known) ____________________

Time of departure ____________________

Time of arrival __________ Airport __________

Contact address (if known) ____________________

____

__________ Tel. __________

Date of return ____________________

Time of return ____________________

In England Mr Petrides will be using his credit card to pay for the car.

VISUM

EXPIRES	CODE	CARD No
May 198-	SU-69-X	H89472-B

NAME
Mr. Spiros C. Petrides

SIGNATURE
Spiros Petrides.

and of course he will need his driving licence.

REPUBLIC OF CYPRUS
Private Driving Licence

Name SPIROS PETRIDES

Date of birth 6 JULY 1947

Home address SALAMIS 49 NICOSIA

Date of issue 14 NOVEMBER 1969

Date of expiry 5 JULY 2017

Licence no. 2 - 48230

Look at the opposite page: *occupation* = post

Write 'NO' here

Reservation form

Please reserve the following Nelson car for me:

On ______________________ (date)
At ______________________ (time)
For ______________________ (days)
From group ______________ (1st choice)
Or group_________________ (2nd choice)

Please deliver to ______________
Collect from ________________

I will be arriving on:
Flight no. ________ From __________
Scheduled to arrive at ____________ (time)

To help eliminate any delay when you collect your Nelson car, please complete the details below as accurately as possible.

Name and initials ________________
Occupation ______________________
Permanent address _______________
____
_______________________ Tel. no. ________
Method of payment — if credit card:
Type ___________________________
No. and expiry date _______________
Driving licence no. _______________
Expires _________________________
U.K. contact address (if known) ________
____
_______________________ Tel. no. ________

Insurance proposal

Driver's date of birth ______________
Length of licence held (years) _________
Occupation ______________________

If you wish more than one person to drive, please give the following details on a separate sheet.

Convictions in the last 5 years ________
____
Accidents in the last 3 years _________
____
Has any insurance company cancelled or declined to renew a policy of the drivers ___
____
Have you any disability which could affect cover ___________________________
____

Additional requirements

Roof rack ________________________
Child seat ________________________
Continental/Irish touring_____________
Ferry bookings_____________________

Exact name of airport

Home address

Convictions means punishment for dangerous or drunken driving

Disability means a problem like very bad eyesight, hearing

6 Vocabulary exercise

PAYMENT A mini-dictionary

price a general word. How much you pay for something, what you pay in a shop, restaurant etc.
What's the price of these shoes?

cost of goods (especially of producing goods), and transport, insurance, organisation. The cost of running a hotel.
The cost of air transport is very high.

rate cost of hiring something, for a period of time. A weekly rate for hiring a car.
The rate for hiring this boat is £2 an hour.

rent used especially for hiring a flat, a house.
The rent of this holiday flat is £150 a week.

charge [1]usually the cost of something extra, not included in the main price.
A small charge is made for the use of the swimming pool.
Look at the bottom of p. 19. There are extra charges for these additional requirements.
[2]the cost of service (= when someone does something for you).
There is a 15% service charge.

Fee cost of a professional service, especially a doctor's or lawyer's fees. For a school, 'tuition fees' (see p. 25) means the cost of lessons (tuition = teaching).
It's a very good school, but the fees are very high.

tariff a list of all the different prices. On p. 18 there is a tariff of car hire rates.

Now read this conversation and fill in the blanks. Two students in London are talking.

Let's hire a rowing boat on the lake. There's a ______ there. We'll see what the hourly ______ is.

Well, Maria, what do you think of ______ in general in London?

Some are high. The ______ of food in a good restaurant, for example. The menu looks cheap, but don't forget they add 15% VAT and a 10% service ______. But the ______ of transport isn't too high, especially if you have a London Transport pass. And taxis are quite cheap.

True, but the ______ of my flat is quite a lot, and there is also an extra ______ for heating in winter, and when I leave there will be a cleaning ______. But I think the telephone is cheap. The Sunday ______ for a minute to my country is very low. And I had to go to the dentist's once. He pulled a tooth out. His ______ were not too bad. And I think the tuition ______ at my school are reasonable, too, because the ______ of running a school in London must be enormous. On the other hand, the ______ of a soft drink is pretty high, if you buy it in the street.

How do you pay?

Usually for small amounts you pay *cash.*

For other methods we say BY.

He paid the hotel bill *by cheque.*
Mr Petrides is going to pay *by credit card.*
Payment, in sterling, is to be made *by letter of credit.*

When do you pay?

If you pay before you receive the goods or services, you pay IN ADVANCE.

The whole cost of hiring a car is payable *in advance.*

Often when you make a reservation you must pay a DEPOSIT.
For example, if you go to a language school in England you usually pay a £50 deposit when you book. The rest, or the BALANCE, is payable when you arrive at the school. Sometimes the deposit is NON-RETURNABLE, that means you do not get it back if you don't go.

For a service, like having your offices redecorated, you usually pay ON COMPLETION, that means, when the job is completed, finished.

If you are very late with your payment, you are IN ARREARS.
(This is dealt with in Unit 8).

7 Active and Passive

The use of the passive with modals:

will/would, shall/should, can/could, must/have to, may/might

Example: ACTIVE You should make payment by cheque.
PASSIVE Payment should *be made* by cheque.

1 You must arrange payment through your bank.

____

2 We can send the goods by air.

____

3 You have to pack the machine carefully.

____

4 You may arrange transport through our agents.

____

5 You must show your driving licence when you hire a car.

____

6 We will deliver the goods next week.

____

8 Vocabulary exercise

Words in *-ion*

A Words in *-ation*

In this unit there are a lot of pairs of words like this:

verb: TO INFORM	noun: INFORMATION
TO RESERVE	RESERVATION

Find the nouns from the verbs given. If the verb is not in this unit it is in brackets (***Occupy***).

1	***Install***	Mr Turan is interested in the ________________ of a new switchboard.
2	***Confirm***	We are waiting for ________________ of their booking.
3	***Quote***	We are happy to submit our ________________.
4	(***Occupy***)	Mr Petrides's job is sales manager. This is his ________________.
5	(***Converse***)	We refer to our telephone ________________ of yesterday.

There are also three verbs in *-ATE* in this unit. Make the noun yourself.

6	***Accommodate***	Mrs Ethel James is looking for a flat. She doesn't want hotel ________________.
7	***Indicate***	The buyer gives you exact ________________ about how the goods should be packed.
8	***Hesitate***	Mr Petrides decides to chose the Nelson offer without ________________.

B Now find the two nouns in *-TION.*

9	***Collect***	Wiley's car hire offers a car delivery and ________________ service for a small extra charge.
10	***Complete***	You usually pay for a service on ________________ of the work.

C Now look at the two in *-IDE* → *-ISION.*

11 In case you ***Collide*** with another car you take out an insurance called ________________ Damage Waiver.

12 Mr Petrides ***Decides*** to accept the Nelson offer. That is his ________________.

9 Dictation

Little words out of big words

HESITATION How many smaller words can you find in this word? Each letter can be used once only in your word.

A tip – arrange your words in columns, alphabetically. Example.

A	E	H	I	N	O	S	T
a	eat		it				

If you find 10 words, good. 20 words, very good. 30 words, excellent.

Back up task

Now use all the points in this unit to write the following exchange of letters.

The language school

You want to study English at a language school in England for three weeks. Look at this advertisement in your local newspaper and choose the course you would like to go on.

Learn English

In one of the most beautiful parts of the country!

We offer GENERAL and INTENSIVE Summer courses

NEW THIS YEAR ENGLISH and FOOTBALL
ENGLISH and COMPUTER STUDIES

Small classes, family accommodation.

Write now to: *Mr L. Morris, The Principal, Colwall College, Malvern, Worcs WR13 6DU.*

1 Write asking for a quotation for three weeks, staying in a family. Give the dates of your stay. Ask for an enrolment form.

2 The principal of the language school replies.

He thanks you.
He gives you a quotation (mentioning tuition, accommodation and extras).
He encloses a prospectus and enrolment form.
He says that there is a £30 deposit payable.
He says the fees are payable in advance.

Write his letter using the information given below.

Colwall College (Prices 198-) All prices are per week

TUITION FEES

General English	15 hours per week	**£50**
Intensive English	20 hours per week	**£65**
English and Football	12 hours English, 10 hours football	**£60**
English and Computers	12 hours English, 10 hours computers	**£70**

ACCOMMODATION

Family accommodation in single room, with bed, breakfast and evening meal **£50**
Student Hostel, shared room with bed and breakfast **£30**
Guest House, single room with bed and breakfast **£70**

The above prices INCLUDE all books and materials and VAT at 15%.

Not included: Excursions
Collection from Heathrow or Gatwick Airport **£30**

Please note: *non-returnable* deposit of £30 is payable on enrolment.
The balance is payable in advance on arrival at the school.

Unit 4

Arranging a business trip

1 As we have already seen, Mr Spiros Petrides will be going to England on business in November. He has spent a long time planning his trip, which is to promote sales of Cyprus Tinned Fruit. A lot of letters have been written to arrange appointments with his clients. Now his itinerary is ready. Listen to the cassette and fill in the rest of the form.

New instruction: Leave blank = don't write anything.

Cyprus Agricultural Development Board

Name ______________________________

Country ______________________________

Date	Destination	Hotel	Appointments	Executive	Time
Nov. 10					
Nov. 11					
Nov. 12					
Nov. 13					
Nov. 14					
Nov. 15					
Nov. 16					

2 Booking hotel accommodation

Building up the letter

Perhaps the executive will write the letter in his own name, or he will ask his secretary to write it on his behalf (= for him).

I Our Sales Manager, Our Director, Mr .... Our Export Manager,	will be visiting	London England Japan Turkey	on business in	November. January. the near future.

Write two sentences.

I would be grateful glad	if you could reserve a	single room double room	for	him/me him/me and his/my wife	from 10–15 December. for the 10, 11 and 16 November.

Write two sentences.

Please Could you	confirm this booking and let us know	your terms. the full cost.

Write one sentence.

3 Now write Elena's letter to the Plaza Hotel in London. Remember to say that you look forward to hearing from them.

4 Confirming a booking

This is the reply Elena got from the Plaza Hotel.

Plaza Hotel

Plaza Hotel — Lancaster Gate — London WC

18 September 198-

Miss E. Stergis
Cyprus Agricultural Development Board
Nicosia
Cyprus

Dear Miss Stergis

We acknowledge receipt of your letter of 14th September.

We are happy to reserve a single room for Mr S. Petrides for the 10th and 11th November. The reservation will be held until 8 p.m. unless paid for in advance.

The price of the room is £42 a night, service, VAT and continental breakfast included. There is an extra charge for English breakfast. All rooms are fully equipped with telephone, television and minibar.

If we do not hear to the contrary, we shall assume that this booking is definite and look forward to receiving Mr Petrides.

Yours sincerely

And this is the letter of confirmation which Elena wrote to Nelson Cars.

Cyprus Agricultural Development Board

22 September 198-

Nelson Cars
15 Elgar Avenue
Hounslow
Middlesex
England

Dear Mr Nelson

Thank you for your letter of 14 September.

This is to confirm that I would like to hire a Group D car from 10 - 16 November 198-.

Please find enclosed my booking form. If you need any further information do not hesitate to write.

Unless I hear to the contrary, I shall assume that the reservation is confirmed.

Yours sincerely

Elena Stergis

pp Spiros Petrides
Sales Manager

Enc

5 Building up the letter

There are two new items here.

A

This is to confirm I/We hereby confirm I am happy to confirm	my booking of our reservation of		a room in your hotel . . . a holiday flat in . . .
	that I would like to	reserve/book	a seat on flight . . .
		enrol in	a language course . . .

Write two sentences like this.

When you have confirmed your booking you think that everything should now be all right. We write a sentence like this.

B

If we do not Unless we	hear	to the contrary, from you,	we shall assume that	the booking is confirmed. this is definite. this is convenient.

Write one sentence.

6

This is Mrs Ethel James's letter of confirmation for the two-room flat in Ibiza. Unfortunately someone spilled Tippex all over it and she had to type it out again. Can you fill in the blanks?

Thank you   your letter of 25th June.

I have dec   to take the two   fl   in Ibiza

from 6th – 20th S

I enc   my b   f   and a ch

for £50 as a dep   .

If I do not   you, I s   as   that the

res   is def   and I shall contact you nearer

the date of departure for further details.

Yours sincerely

Ethel James.

7 On the letters on pp. 16 and 28 you will find the initials p.p.(pp) next to the sender's name.

This means that the secretary has signed the letter 'for' her boss or on his behalf.

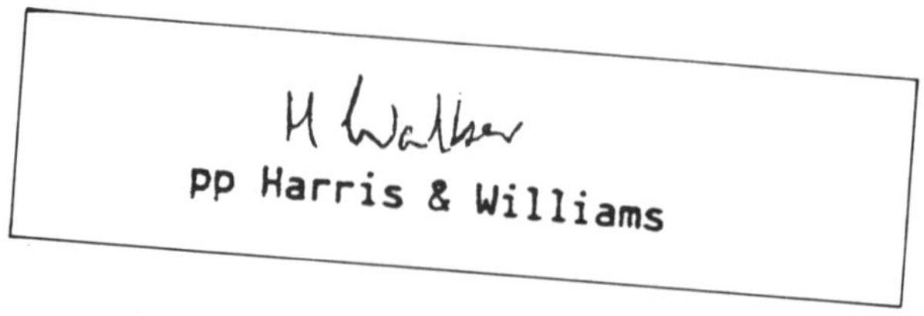

On behalf of also means 'for'. It is used with the possessive/genitive.

Example: for me = *on* **my** *behalf.*
for him = *on* **his** *behalf.*
for the company = *on* **the company's** *behalf*; or *on behalf* **of the company.**

Now you do it.

For them = ______________________ For us = ______________________

For Mr Smith = ______________________ or ______________________

8 Arranging a business appointment

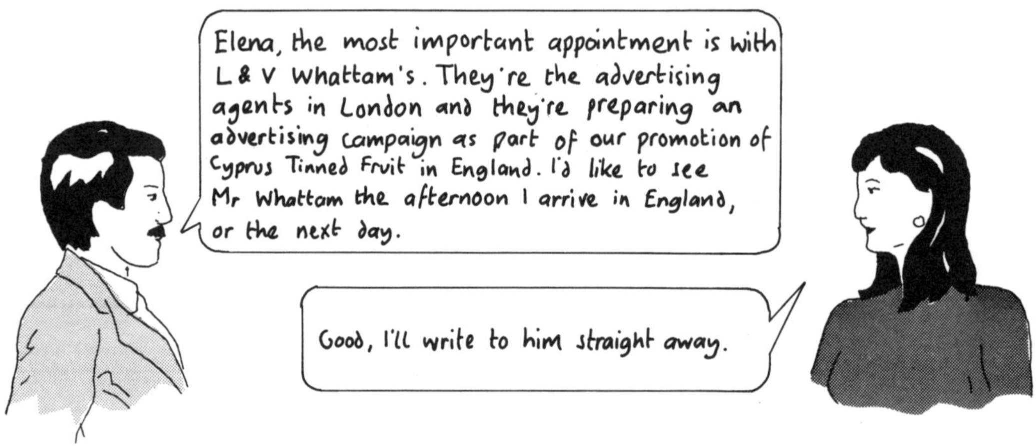

Building up the letter

A You can use the same sentence as for booking hotel accommodation on p. 27 or:

I Our Sales Manager, Mr . . .	will be spending	two weeks three days one month	in	Europe the Far East Liverpool (your country)	in	November. March. the summer.

Write two sentences like this.

____

____

____

____

B Give the exact dates and mention any person you want to see, or project that has to be discussed.

I He	will be in	London Athens Tokyo	on 6 June from 12–15 January	and would like to

arrange an appointment with	you your Sales Manager your Marketing Manager your Personnel Officer

to discuss	the advertising campaign for Cyprus Tinned Fruit. the sales of our office equipment. the staff exchange scheme. your planned visit to Japan.

Write two sentences.

C

Please let us know whether We hope that	this will be convenient for you.

Write one sentence.

9 Write Elena's letter to L & V Whattam Ltd.

10 Dictation

New word: suggest = propose

11 The future continuous

When we want to talk about something that will happen at an exact point in the future, we often use the *future continuous*.

Example: Our export manager will BE visitING Japan next February.

The future continuous is formed with *will/shall* + *be* + *ing*

Rewrite these sentences using the *future continuous*.

Example: This time tomorrow/I/discuss/advertising campaign.
This time tomorrow I will be discussing our advertising campaign.

1 4 June / director / fly / New York

____

2 The engineers/ install /switchboard / Istanbul / next week

____

3 Mr Petrides / promote / Cyprus Fruit / when / go / England

____

4 He / have lunch / Mr Ellis / 13.00 / Friday

____

5 I / meet / him / airport / tomorrow afternoon

____

12 if not = unless

Instead of saying 'If . . . not' we can also say 'unless'.

If we do not Unless we	hear from you	Be careful with he / she / it	If he does not come Unless he comes

Now change the underlined part of the sentence.

1 If he does not want to discuss the project, he needn't come to the meeting.

____

2 Unless he has booked a seat, he can't take flight CY422.

____

3 We cannot accept their booking if they haven't paid a deposit.

____

4 I'm afraid you can't see the director unless you make an appointment.

____

13 Vocabulary exercise

FLUFFITOYS Pty.

298 Malvern Road, Melbourne, Australia
Tel. 062 79 42 Telex AB 94432

Complete the passage with all the words from the box. You must put the word in the correct form.

agent
appointment
assume
campaign
contrary
convenient
definite
destination
discuss
executive
itinerary
promote
trip
unless

Lewis Davison, sales manager of Fluffitoys Pty of Melbourne, Australia, will be going to Japan next October to __________ his company's products.
He has already made several __________ to meet important business __________ in the toy business all over Japan. In Tokyo he is first going to __________ the advertising __________ with his advertising __________.
He also has many other __________, including Nagoya, Osaka and Kyoto, on his __________.
He is lucky: all the times for meetings which he suggested were __________, and because the hotels are not full in October he was able to make __________ bookings without any problems. So his business __________ is now all well planned, and he can __________ that everything will be fine, __________ he hears anything to the __________ before he goes.

14 Vocabulary exercise

Find the noun from the verb given in CAPITALS.

1 If you can't PAY cash, you can make __________ by cheque.
2 If you want to ENROL for a course, fill in the __________ form.
3 Elena ARRANGED the business trip. She made all the __________.
4 The hotel room is fully EQUIPPED. There is a lot of __________.
5 Some people who hire a car don't REQUIRE a roof rack. It is an additional __________ for people with lots of luggage.
6 An ADVERTISING agent's job is to make __________.
7 They haven't ACKNOWLEDGED receipt of our letter yet. We are still waiting for an __________.

Have you noticed? In the singular all the nouns end in -__________

There are FOUR other words with this ending used in this book up till now. Can you find them all? Answers on p.47.

__________ __________

__________ __________

15 Verbs and prepositions

Many of the verbs used so far have a preposition (or adverb particle) after them. Here is a list. Some of them are used several times.

ABOUT BACK FOR FORWARD FROM IN ON OUT TO

In this exercise you must fill ___ the blanks.

1 I am looking ______ ______ hearing from you.
2 The fluffy elephants were so successful that they all sold ______ in a short time. The shop had to ask ______ some more.
3 A non-returnable deposit is one which you don't get ______.
4 I refer ______ the telephone conversation we had yesterday.
5 Mrs Ethel James is looking ______ a flat in a quiet place. She is interested ______ going to Ibiza.
6 At the Plaza Hotel an English breakfast is not included ______ the price. You must pay extra ______ it.
7 Mr Turan is having a new switchboard put ______ in his hotel.
8 I have heard ______ your school ______ a business friend, and I would like to enrol ______ a month's summer course.
9 If you write a word wrong in a dictation, cross it ______ and write it again.
10 Next week the busy executive is going ______ a business trip and then he's going ______ a three-day computer course.

16 Hidden words

There are twenty words, all in this unit, hidden here. Can you find them? 11 are across, 6 are down and 3 are diagonal. They all have at least four letters.

3–7 words, good. 8–14 words, very good. 15–20 words, excellent.
Answers on p. 41.

A	C	K	N	O	W	L	E	D	G	E	B	E	H	A	L	F	D	D
E	O	O	J	Z	X	B	B	L	A	N	K	U	M	N	P	I	X	E
L	N	U	N	L	E	S	S	X	S	A	L	E	S	C	O	T	A	S
E	T	T	B	V	F	F	T	J	S	K	G	A	I	I	Z	I	H	U
P	R	I	C	E	E	X	E	C	U	T	I	V	E	X	N	N	P	G
H	A	B	O	W	Y	N	G	V	M	I	E	E	X	K	W	E	L	G
A	R	D	E	F	I	N	I	T	E	M	P	R	Q	O	T	R	S	E
N	Y	E	Z	U	E	N	Z	E	C	E	A	P	M	J	I	A	Y	S
T	X	C	A	M	P	A	I	G	N	O	F	F	J	S	U	R	K	T
S	T	A	F	F	Z	V	L	L	U	T	R	I	P	D	Y	Y	O	Q

17 Correction exercise

Sir V. Rich, the multimillionaire, is a brilliant businessman, but he's always been terrible at spelling and he can't even type properly.

As his chauffeur-driven Rolls Royce sped towards London one Monday morning he suddenly had that Monday morning feeling, like the rest of us!

He had forgotten a very important business letter which had to be sent off first thing. He got out his portable computerised typewriter, or word processor, and started typing furiously. This was the result as it appeared on the screen.
First guess how many words are wrong, then correct them yourself.

Deaf sit
I acknowlege reciept of your leter of 2th may.

I am very happy two here of your intrest in out TRIDENT rang of prodcuts and i am delithged that you May try to markit them inn yore countree.

I note that yoy are planing too bee in London form 3rd to 10th Juen. Unforchunatly I will be away on buisness myself untill the 8th, so I wood sugest that you cum to my office at 10 o'colck on Tuseday 9th. Wee will certainly disscus the possibillities of a sails campaing to promote hour gods and I hop that our adventising manger will be present at the meating.

Pleeze let me no weather this will be convinient for you.

Yoars fatfully

Fortunately for Sir Vernon Rich, however, his word processor had an automatic correcting programme, so the print-out of the letter was perfect.

Even his secretary was pleased with him!

Back up task

1 A night in Nagoya

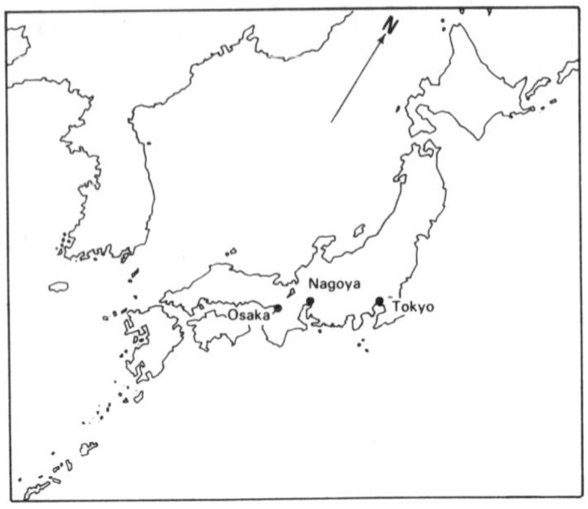

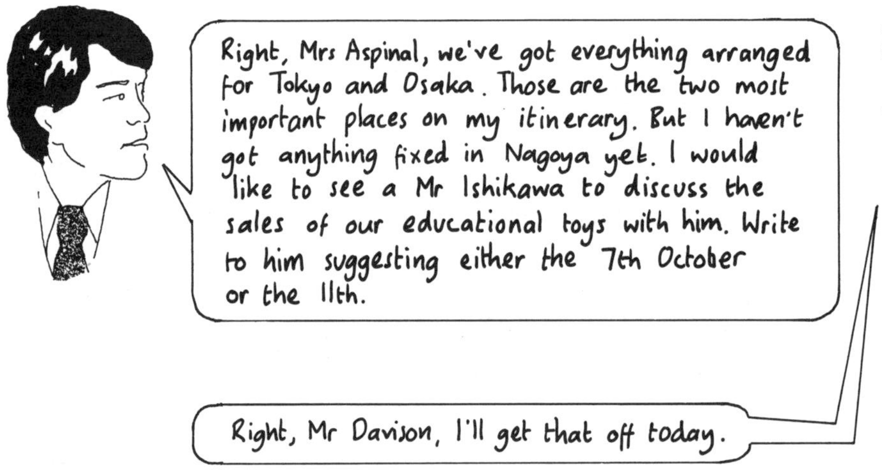

Two weeks later

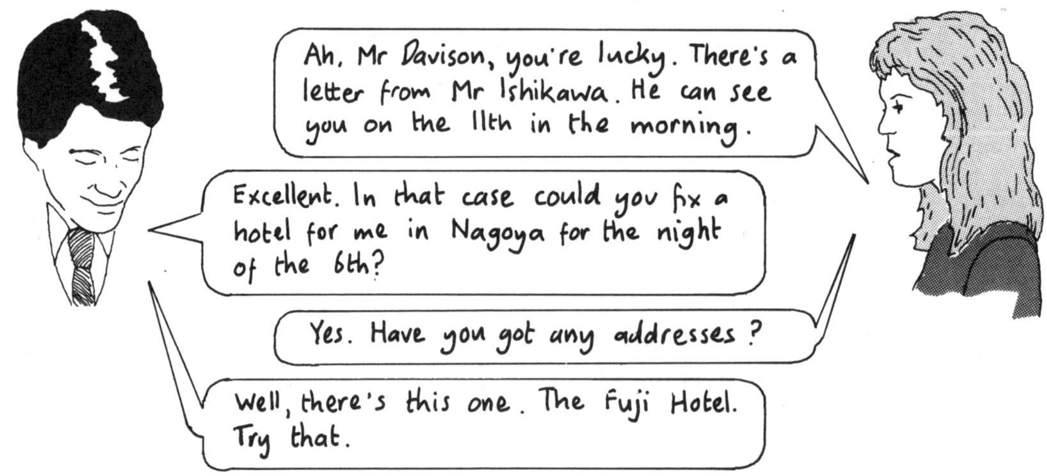

2 Look at p. 25 again.

You have decided to go to Colwall College to learn English.

Write a letter confirming that you would like to enrol for a three week course.

Enclose your enrolment form and an IMO (International Money Order) for the £30 deposit.

Use the Build Up section on p. 29 to help you.

Unit 5

Sales letters – Counter-proposals

1 Sometimes a company trying to market a new product writes a *sales letter* to hundreds of customers to attract their attention. Mrs Teroko Takada, manageress of a perfume shop in Tokyo receives this letter from Italy.

Our ref GA/1/87

Cosmafarma

29 via Mascagni
00146 ROMA
Italy

tel 728771
tx 612515

Mrs T. Takada
The Manageress
Lucky Star Boutique
Sendai Building
6-1-2 Shiba-koen
Minato-ku
Tokyo
Japan

Dear Madam

As a regular stockist of our exclusive Giotto perfumes, you will be pleased to hear that we have developed a new line, the

<u>Giotto Amore</u>

which we are now promoting worldwide with great success.

We have great pleasure in making you a special introductory offer of 100 sets of Amore (to include perfume, toilet water, soap and body lotion) in beautifully-designed display packages.

The price is only $30 each.

You will soon receive sample bottles of the new perfume and we are sure that once your customers have tried it they will change over to this line.

We look forward to hearing your own opinion of Amore and to receiving your order, which will be dealt with promptly.

Yours faithfully

Giovanni Di Pietro

Giovanni Di Pietro
Sales Manager

2 Sometimes you get an offer for products which you would like to stock. But you don't like the terms of the offer. You feel the price is too high, the discount is not large enough, or the delivery time too long. Or there are a lot of similar products on the market and you want an extra discount because another new product might be difficult to sell. Look at Mrs Takada's reaction to Cosmafirma's sales letter.

3 This type of letter is called a **counter-proposal.**

Building up the letter.

A Say that you have received the sales letter/samples.

(a) Mention any *advantages* of the product.

Thank you for We have received	the samples of	Giotto 'Amore'. your chocolate. the new fruit juice. 'Laura' writing paper.

The quality is excellent. We are very satisfied with the high quality. The colours are very attractive. The taste is delicious.

Write two sentences like this.

____

____

____

____

(b) Or perhaps you have had a demonstration of a machine, or have used it for a trial period.

We have now tried out Thank you for letting us try out Thank you for demonstrating	the your	'Falcon' 25 typewriter 'Wasp' lawn mower 'Timbermate' electric saw

, which we find attractive and easy to use. We are very satisfied with its performance.

Write two sentences like this.

____

____

____

____

B Now mention the *disadvantages.*

However, we would like to point out we must mention	that there is strong competition in	this field the office equipment market the food industry

(and)

Japanese / American / German producers The Japanese / Americans / Germans	offer similar products at lower prices.
We have received better offers from other producers. Your competitors offer better terms.	

Write two sentences like this. Join them with 'and'.

____

____

____

____

C Your proposal

(*a*) Perhaps the price is too high.

Business in this market is very slack The dollar is very high at the moment Your prices are too high for our market

and we can, therefore, only accept your offer

with a 5% reduction in the prices quoted. if you grant us a 10% discount. if you increase your discount from 5% to 10%.

Write two sentences.

____

____

____

____

____

____

(*b*) Perhaps the number of articles you have to buy is too large.

Your minimum	offer quantity	of	100 sets ten lawnmowers 1500 litres 50 kilos	is too large.

We could only place an order for	50 sets. six lawnmowers. 1200 litres. 40 kilos.

Write a sentence like this.

D You hope they agree and you offer hope of further orders.

We	hope trust	you will agree to our proposal and assure you that,

if the	electric saws typewriters perfume	sell(s) well, we will place	further repeat	orders.

Write a sentence like this.

4 Now write the letter for Mrs Takada.

Answers to hidden words.

A	C	K	N	O	W	L	E	D	G	E	B	E	H	A	L	F	D	D
E	O	O	J	Z	X	B	B	L	A	N	K	U	M	N	P	I	X	E
L	N	U	N	L	E	S	S	X	S	A	L	E	S	C	O	T	A	S
E	T	T	B	V	F	F	T	J	S	K	G	A	I	I	Z	I	H	U
P	R	I	C	E	E	X	E	C	U	T	I	V	E	X	N	N	P	G
H	A	B	O	W	Y	N	G	V	M	I	E	E	X	K	W	E	L	G
A	R	D	E	F	I	N	I	T	E	M	P	R	Q	O	T	R	S	E
N	Y	E	Z	U	E	N	Z	E	C	E	A	P	M	J	I	A	Y	S
T	X	C	A	M	P	A	I	G	N	O	F	F	J	S	U	R	K	T
S	T	A	F	F	Z	V	L	L	U	T	R	I	P	D	Y	Y	O	Q

5 The reply is often a compromise between the initial offer and your counter-proposal.

Cosmafarma

29 via Mascagni
00146 ROMA
Italy

tel 728771
tx 612515

Our ref GA/1/87
Your ref TT/yo

Mrs T. Takada
The Manageress
Lucky Star Boutique
Sendai Building
6-1-2 Shiba-koen
Minato-ku
Tokyo
Japan

Dear Mrs Takada

Thank you for your letter of ...

We are delighted that you have tried the new Giotto Amore and would like to stock it.

We have considered your proposal carefully and, since you are a valued customer, we would be prepared to let you have a 10% introductory discount on an order of 75 sets, or 5% on an order of 50.

You will realise that these prices are already very competitive for this high quality and that it would hardly be worthwhile for us to sell in smaller quantities.

We hope you will agree to one of these suggestions and look forward to receiving your order.

Yours sincerely

Giovanni Di Pietro

Giovanni Di Pietro
Sales Manager

Which offer do you think Mrs Takada accepts?

6 Dictation

Vocabulary exercise

In this unit there are many words beginning with per- and pr-. Do you know them? Fill in the squares under these sentences.

1 You should reply to a letter . . .
2 You try out a machine for a trial . . .
3 'Amore' is the name of a . . .
4 Mrs Takada made a counter- . . .
5 The price is too high . . . (= maybe).
6 Mr Di Pietro wrote hundreds of sales letters to . . . his goods.
7 We would be . . . (= ready) to let you have a 10% discount.
8 The Americans, Japanese and Germans are all . . . (= makers) of cars.
9 The machine *performed* well. It gave a good . . .

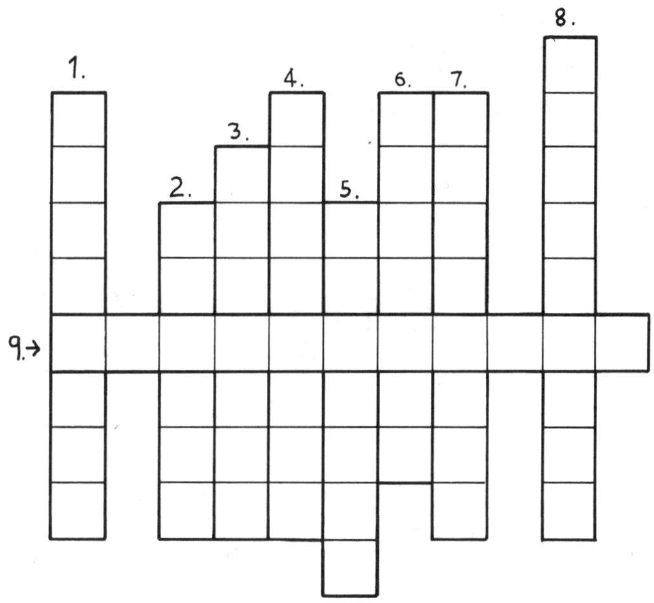

7 **To compete (with)** means to do business against another company, to try to sell more goods.
'Coca-Cola competes with Pepsi-Cola.'

The company (or a person) is the competitor (noun, countable).

Many companies selling similar products means there is competition (noun, uncountable).

The situation becomes very competitive (adjective) (= hard to sell goods), and prices also become competitive (= lower).

Fill in the right form of **compete**.

The Personal Computer business
Any company wanting to __________ in the PC market must know that there are already a lot of __________, for example IBM, Commodore and Apple. Because of all this strong __________, prices have to be very __________ or you will not sell. So, if you are going to enter this __________ market, you must be able to __________ with your __________, who will not like you to sell cheaply in a market where there is already enough hard __________. They will probably buy up your company very quickly.

Dear Student You are now half way through the book. Have a laugh!

8 Vocabulary exercise

Form the next word from the one given in CAPITALS.

Marketing goods

Some goods are easier to PROMOTE than others, for example, the Giotto 'Amore', whose ____________ is very SUCCESSFUL at the moment. One reason for this ____________ is certainly that the display packages are very ATTRACTIVE in order to ____________ customers' attention, but another is that to INTRODUCE the new perfume onto the market, Cosmafirma is making a cheap ____________ offer.

As sales manager, all Mr Di Pietro has to do to make sure that it is in STOCK in shops is to write to all his ____________ and send them samples.

It is much more difficult to market goods like machines, where customers who want to TRY out a model have to have one on ____________, or where they want someone to DEMONSTRATE how it works. Then the company has to send someone to give a ____________.

9 The Cinderella words

If you don't know who Cinderella was, ask your teacher!

In Units 4 and 5 there are a lot of new words like *appointment*, *advertising*, *competition* which are mentioned several times.
But there are also many other new words which are only mentioned once.
Do you know what they are? They mean the same as the words in **bold type**, and the first letter is given.

1 Chocolate is eaten **all over the world.** It is eaten *w* . . . .

2 Another word for **if** is *w* . . . . . .

3 'Amore' was very successful **at first**. It had great *i* . . . . . . success.

4 In a seaside town there is **not much** business in winter. Business is very *s* . . . .

5 **With this letter** we confirm our reservation. We *h* . . . . . confirm it.

6 We have a **high opinion** of Mrs Takada. She is a *v* . . . . . customer.

7 They were discussing a **project** to sell snow to the Eskimos. Not a very worthwhile *s* . . . . .

8 The minimum offer of perfume was 100 sets. Mrs Takada only wanted 50, but in the end she took **something in the middle**, 75. This was a *c* . . . .

10 Negotiating

Listen to this conversation and fill in the information on the table below.

Name of customer ______________________________

____

The customer is

a) regular and buys a lot ☐
b) not very regular buts buys a lot ☐
c) regular but doesn't buy much ☐
d) not regular and doesn't buy much ☐

Type of product ______________________________

____

Name of product ______________________________

Name of designer

a) Terino ☐
b) Torini ☐
c) Delini ☐

	Original offer	Counter Proposal	Final Offer
Quantity			
Price each			

Terms of payment ______________________________

Now write Jane's letter to the customer. Listen to the conversation again if necessary and use the letter on p.42 to help you.

Did you know?

Did you know that the longest letter ever written is one of 1,113,747 words, written in eight months ending in May 1976, by Jacqueline Jones of Lindale, Texas, USA, to her sister.

This book, *Take Another Letter*, probably has about 22,500 words, so Mrs Jones's letter is almost exactly 50 times longer, in other words, make a pile of 50 *Take Another Letter* and you can see how big Mrs Jones's letter was.

And now, if you want to beat Mrs Jones's record, START WRITING!!

Back up task

1 You receive the following offer.

Dear Customer,

The Easifix Range of Electric Staplers

This is the latest in electric staplers!

We are introducing three new models to solve every stapling problem. Don't miss our special introductory offer:

The pocket-size **A50** — the lightning stapler for private and office use.

The medium **A100** — staples up to 20 pages.

The large **B100** heavy duty stapler — staples up to 100 pages, also highly suitable for wood.

Discount of 5% on orders over 50
Discount of 10% on orders over 100

All these models are available in five attractive colours and staples come in boxes of 500, 1000 and 5000.

For further details look at our enclosed brochure and price list and choose the models you want for a trial period of one month. We *know* you will be satisfied!

Yours faithfully

J. Small

2 You have these models on trial and make a counter-proposal. Write your letter based on these ideas. Look at pp. 39–41 to help.

A (The advantages) The quality is high, the colours are very attractive. The staplers are easy to use.
B (The disadvantages) Competition in the field of office equipment is very strong. German and Swedish producers offer lower prices.
C (Your proposal) A 10% reduction on an order of 30 of each model.
D Say you hope to place further orders if the staplers sell well.

ANSWER to p. 33. What are the other words ending in *-MENT*?

appointment (p. 26) development (p. 15) department (p. 4)
document (p. 20)

Unit 6

Making a complaint

1 Of course, between the time you place your order and the time you finally receive your goods, a lot of things can go wrong. Mistakes are made, orders are forgotten or lost, fires and floods destroy goods in warehouses, strikes stop production, goods are stolen and ships sink. Sometimes the goods arrive safely, but are defective.

One day, Mr Tsakos, manager of Apollos Department Store in Athens, is going round the store making sure everything is ready for the Christmas period. He's talking to members of his staff about things which have gone wrong.

9.00	Stationery Department

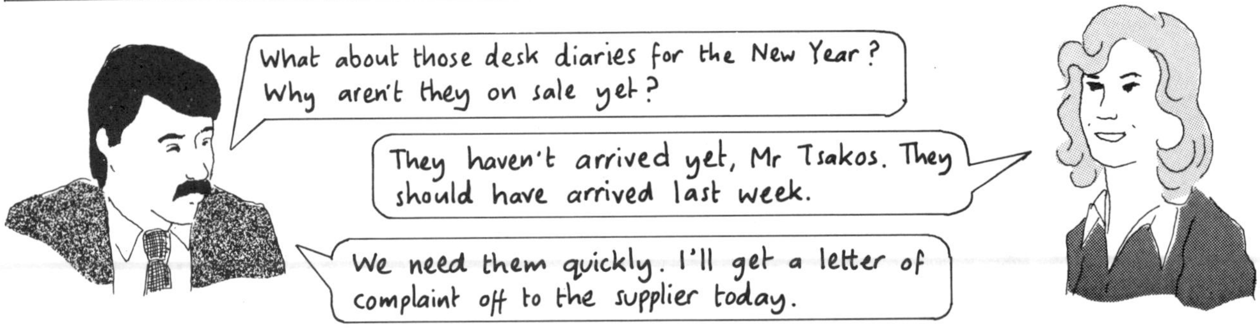

9.30	Toy Department

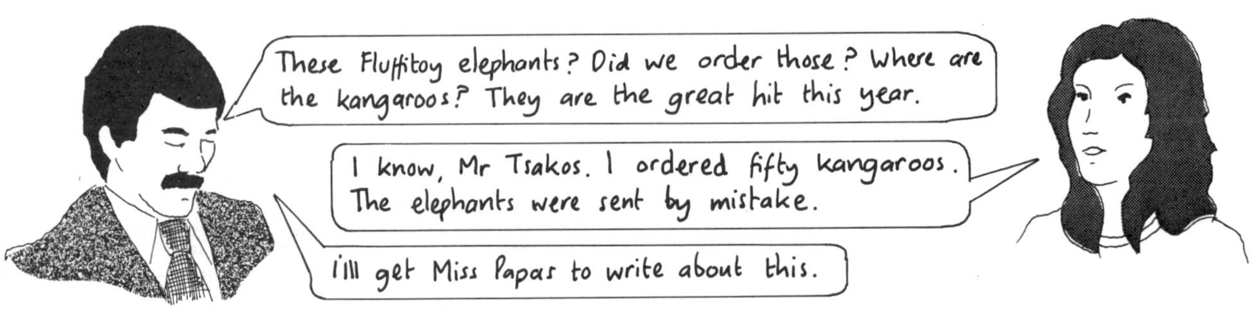

10.00	Clothes Department

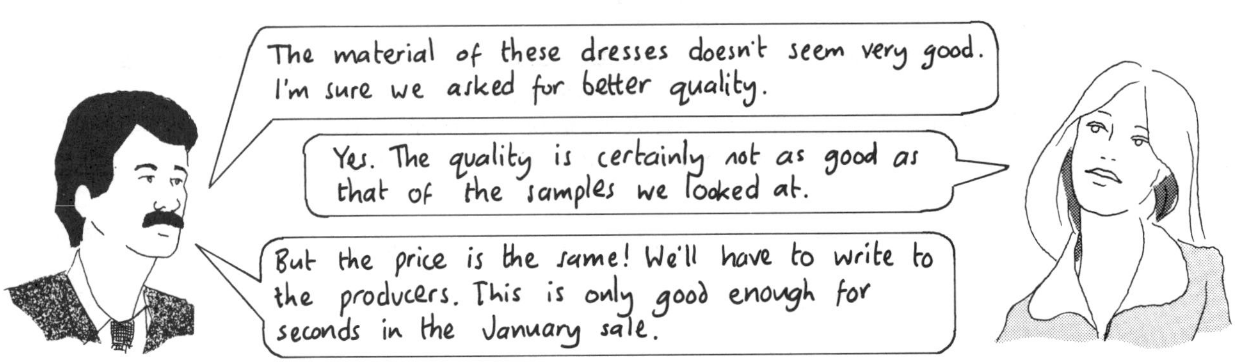

10.30 Household Department

Oh, Mr Tsakos. It's about these copper pans. They're excellent quality, but they've sent too many large ones and not enough small ones.

I see. How many should there be?

25 each. But they've sent 40 large and only 10 small.

They probably mixed up the orders. I'll ask Miss Papas to write immediately.

And there's something else. Look at these wine glasses. Most of them are broken.

I can see. They were badly packed. The carton was not strong enough, or something heavy was placed on top. Glasses are very fragile.

They'll have to send replacements by air straight away. Who'll pay?

That's a case for the insurance. I'll get Miss Papas to send a telex this morning.

10.45 Manager's Office

Miss Papas, I'd like you to take four letters of complaint.

Yes, Mr Tsakos.

Some reasons for complaints

2 Building up the letter

Think of the sentences Miss Papas will use for her four letters of complaint and write some of those.

A Refer to the order/date.

You will probably write the order as a heading.

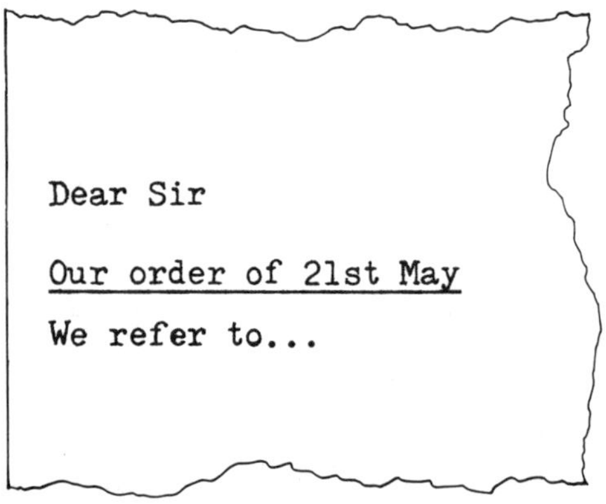
Dear Sir

Our order of 21st May

We refer to...

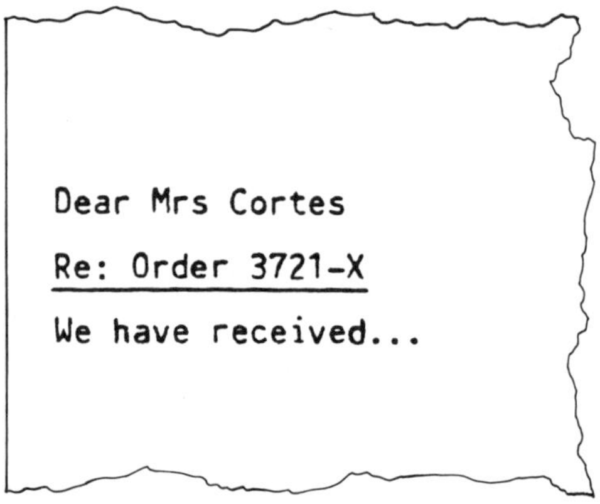
Dear Mrs Cortes

Re: Order 3721-X

We have received...

If you do this, then you can write

We refer to the *above* order / The *above* order has now arrived.

(*a*)

We refer to the	above order desk diaries copper pans electric staplers	which we received today. which we ordered from you in May.

(*b*)

We have now received the The	wine glasses auto spare parts consignment of paint delivery of cameras	which we ordered in May.	has have	now arrived.

Write two sentences like (*a*) and (*b*).

B Mention the general problem. There are many different possibilities here.

(*a*)

Unfortunately	this order has not yet arrived. we have not yet received this order.

Write one of these.

(*b*)

On examining opening	the	consignment order delivery	we noticed that	some of the goods were	broken. badly damaged. defective. missing.
When we examined opened				you did not send us the number	requested. ordered.

Write two sentences like this.

(*c*)

However, when we examined the	dresses stationery paint	we noticed that	the goods are of inferior quality. the quality is inferior to that of the sample you sent us.

Write two sentences like this.

C Point out the exact mistake.

You have sent us fifty fluffy elephants instead of fifty kangaroos.

We asked for twenty size 10 and fifteen size 12. You have sent us five size 10 and twenty-five size 12. Instead of twenty-four large staplers B100 you have sent us only twelve. We expected first quality material. Instead you have sent dresses made of poor quality material.

The goods were not correctly packed and the	glasses have been broken. books have been damaged.

Write two sentences like this for Miss Papas.

____

____

____

____

D Say why you need the goods and ask them to send replacements/the correct goods.

These goods are	required needed	urgently	for	our the	Christmas stock Autumn fashion show January sales coming tourist season
			because		our stocks are running low. we are now out of stock.

and we would ask you to send us the	correct items replacements	as soon as possible. by return of post. without delay.

Write two sentences like this.

____

____

____

____

____

E In serious cases you may have to give a deadline or may even decide to stop doing business with a supplier if he doesn't improve.

If we do not receive the goods by If you are unable to supply us by	1 December the end of the month 31 March
If this happens again	

we regret that we will be obliged to	cancel the order. place future orders elsewhere. look for another supplier.

Write two sentences.

____

____

____

____

____

____

3 Now write two of Miss Papas's letters. First write the letter about the late arrival of the desk diaries, and then any one other.

Item	Number ordered	Date ordered	Received
Ringham Desk Diaries	100	20/9	x
Fluffitoys kangaroos (large)	50	15/8	12/11
'Winter Party' dresses by Fabé	12	14/9	14/11
Kitchen King copper pans large (B12) small (B22)	 25 25	28/9	13/11
'Davinia' cut crystal wineglasses	20 dozen	7/10	15/11

More on ACTIVE and PASSIVE

First, look at pp. 50–54 and see how many passives you can find. Underline them.

A Things that often happen. PRESENT SIMPLE

Example: ACTIVE People make mistakes
PASSIVE Mistakes *are made*

Passive is formed with *is/are* + past participle.

Say what often happens with goods.

1. People send the wrong goods.
2. They forget orders.
3. Someone loses an order.
4. They steal goods.
5. People pack articles badly.
6. They break fragile goods.
7. They don't dispatch the correct items.
8. People mix up orders.

B Something that happened once, last year, or yesterday. PAST SIMPLE.

Example: ACTIVE Someone forgot the order
PASSIVE The order *was forgotten*.

Passive is formed with *was/were* + past participle.

Mr Tsakos is talking to a business friend. Put the conversation into the passive.

Yes, I can tell you we had a lot of problems last year. I remember that . . .

1 People made lots of mistakes and sent inferior material.

____

2 They forgot a lot of orders and didn't pack fragile items well.

____

3 They mixed up several orders and dispatched poor quality dresses.

____

4 People broke some goods and stole other goods

____

5 We wrote dozens of letters of complaint!

____

4 Adverbs

Look at pp. 16-47 again. There are seven adverbs ending in -LY (not counting 'only'). Which are they?

________ ________ ________ ________

________ ________ ________

There are also three others in this unit: **correctly, unfortunately, urgently**.

Adverbs usually tell us about *how* something happens. Fill in the blanks using each of these adverbs once only.

The problem of packing

________, many things can go wrong between the time an order is placed and the time the goods are ________ put on sale.
Some goods have to be packed very carefully, and to make sure that they arrive ________, without any defects, you must give the packers exact instructions for; for packing, like 'fragile', or 'this side up' or 'use no hooks' or 'keep dry'. If you do not, they might pack a fragile item ________. Packers ________ don't make mistakes on purpose, and ________ many mistakes happen because the men have to work ________, especially when an order is required ________.
However, if you do receive damaged goods, the only thing you can do is to inform your suppliers ________ and get them to send replacements, this time ________ packed.

Packing marks

Many packing instructions also have international signs. Which instructions go with which signs?

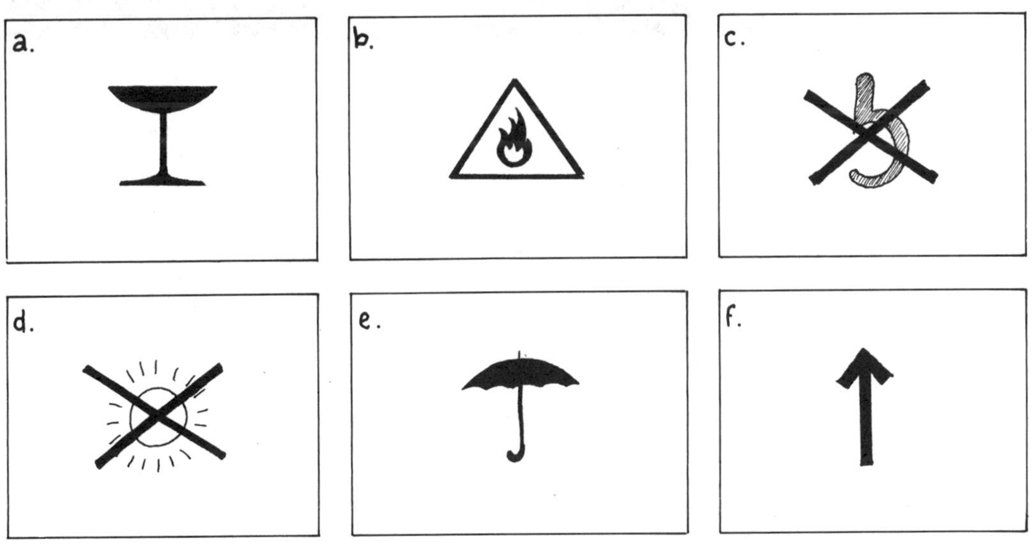

1 This way up ________
2 Keep dry ________
3 Fragile ________
4 Use no hooks ________
5 Perishable (= will not last long, must not be stored near heat, eg fruit) ________
6 Inflammable (= burns easily, eg petrol) ________

5 Crossword

These words are all in this unit. Do you know them?

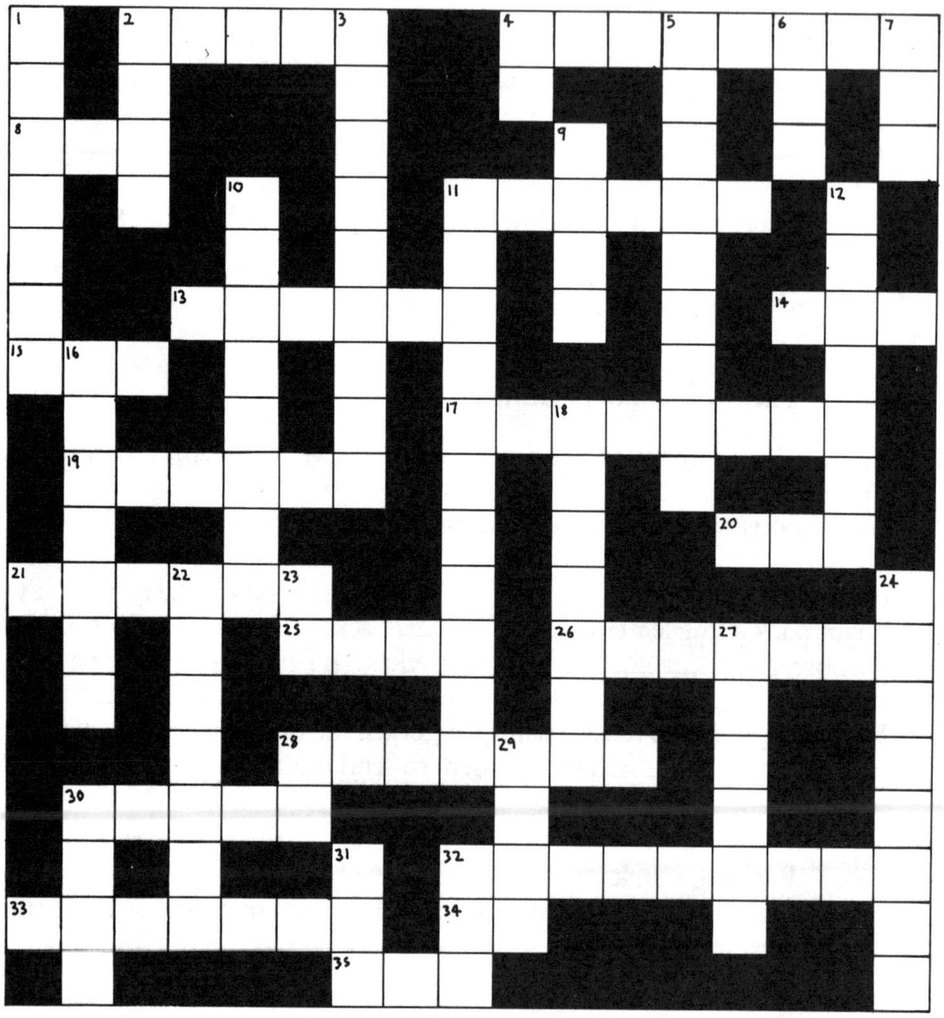

Down

1 We write the dates and times of meetings in these.
2 It burns.
3 If there is something wrong with a machine, it is . . .
4 To mix . . . an order.
5 In another place. With other suppliers.
6 'Something heavy was placed on . . . of the glasses.'
7 'The diaries haven't arrived . . .'
9 'They sent . . . 10 small pans instead of 25.'
10 The latest date when goods must be sent.
11 A delivery of goods.
12 Fire can . . . goods.
16 They sent elephants . . . of kangaroos.
18 Something which breaks easily is . . .
22 Get.
23 'Inferior . . . that of the sample.'
24 A consignment of goods.
27 When you don't have much stock left, your stocks . . . . . . (2 words)
28 (Preposition) . . . a price.
29 Perishable items don't like this.
30 Another word for inferior.
31 The household dep. . .ment.

Across

2 A very great amount of water.
4 'These goods are required . . .' (= very quickly).
8 'They'll have to send replacements by . . . straight away'.
11 If you stop an order you have placed, you . . . it.
13 A thick packing box.
14 Packing instructions. '. . . no hooks.'
15 Dear . . .
17 not good (quality).
19 A . . . may stop production in a factory.
20 Packing instructions. 'Keep . . .'
21 We are sorry. We . . .
25 The past simple is used for things that happened . . .
26 Get better.
28 'We will be obliged to look for . . . supplier.'
30 You use this to redecorate a room.
32 A large building to store goods in.
33 '. . . , when we examined the dresses . . .'
34 Mr Tsakos is in the clothes department . . . 10 o'clock.
35 The fluffy elephants are in the . . . department.

6 Dictation

New punctuation: *Stroke* = / *Question mark* = ?
New word: *Furthermore* = in addition

Sentences with *if* and *unless* for things which will happen.

This sort of sentence (called a conditional) has two parts.
Example:

If we *receive* your order by next week, we *will grant* a 10% discount.

NOTE: We use the *present* tense in the part with *if* or *unless* and (usually) the *future* in the other part (*can/must/need* often take the present)

Write these sentences out in full.

1 If this (happen) again, we (be obliged) to place our orders elsewhere.

2 If the consignment (arrive) late, it (cause) a lot of inconvenience.

3 I (book) the hotel room unless he (tell) me not to.

4 You (have) to replace your switchboard if it (be) getting too old.

5 We (arrange) for a car to meet you if you (let) us know of the time of arrival.

6 If you (return) the damaged goods, we (replace) them immediately.

7 Unless we (hear) from you, we (assume) that this arrangement is convenient.

8 Unless the service (improve), we (start) looking for another supplier.

9 We (cancel) the order if the goods (not/arrive) on time.

10 I think we (go) bankrupt if business (not/improve) soon.

Back up task

1 Look at these businesspeople talking about some problems they have had. Write their letters of complaint.

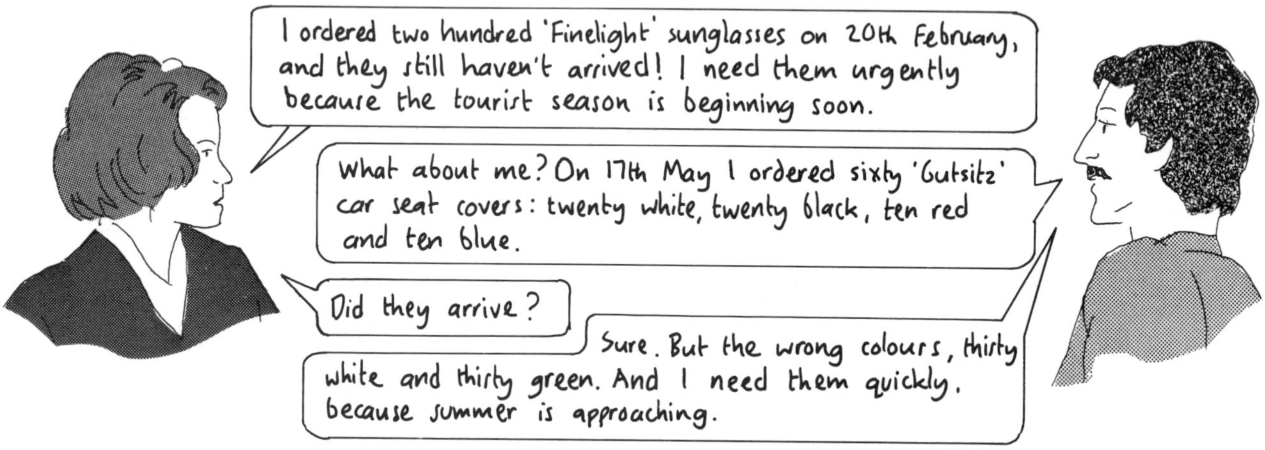

2 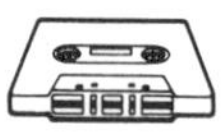 Jim and Harry work in a large London department store. Listen to this conversation about their problems and take notes. Then write their letters of complaint.

Unit 7

Answering a complaint

1 When you receive a letter of complaint you must find out how the mistake was caused and inform your customer straight away. You also tell him what action you are going to take. Perhaps you will have to send him the goods by air to reach him in time. You will also tell the customer to return the wrong goods to you at your expense. However, in some cases, because the cost of packing and forwarding is so high, you may decide it is cheaper to let him keep the wrong goods, but at a much reduced price.

These letters are called *letters of adjustment*.

You must also apologise to your customer for any inconvenience caused. Look at the replies to two of Miss Papas's letters.

Dear Mr Tsakos

Re: Order K490

Thank you for your letter of 15th November, in which you say that you received fifty fluffy elephants instead of the fifty kangaroos you ordered.

We have looked into the matter and found that an error was made in our dispatch department.

The fifty kangaroos have now been sent by air freight and you should receive them within a week.

With regard to the fifty elephants, you can either return them to us (for which we will naturally pay all expenses) or you can keep them for sale. If you decide to do this we will offer a 25% discount on our list price.

We sincerely apologise for any inconvenience caused and hope that you will agree to one of these proposals.

Yours sincerely

Dear Mr Tsakos

100 Ringhams Desk Diaries

We have received your letter of 15th November.

We apologise for the non-arrival of the desk diaries you ordered. This was caused by a strike at our printers. Fortunately the strike is now settled and work has resumed. We have also received the diaries, which were dispatched to you on 16th November. We are sure they will arrive in time to go on sale for Christmas.

Again, we are sorry for any inconvenience caused and hope that this will not happen again.

Yours sincerely

2 Building up the letter

These letters are longer and are built up in four parts.

A You refer to the problem
B You give the reason (if possible)
C You offer to put the matter right
D Somewhere in the letter you must apologise.

A You refer to the problem

We refer to your letter of . . ., in which you say that

the (goods)* (articles)* three of the (machines)*	ordered have not yet arrived. received are not what you ordered. received are defective / faulty.

you received	100 litres of R102 red paint instead of R103. only 15 dresses instead of 25. 20 size 42 rubber boots instead of size 44. 600 bars of chocolate instead of only 60.
the quality of the goods you received is not the same as that of the sample.	

* write the name of the goods etc here

Write three sentences.

B 1 *A delay in delivery.*

If there is a perfectly good reason for the delay, say so, for example, a fire in your warehouse, exceptionally bad weather, floods, a strike, illness among the staff.

(*a*)

This delay was	caused by due to	a strike a dispute industrial action a fire a flood	at our suppliers. at one of our factories. in our workshop. in our warehouse.
		an outbreak of 'flu among our staff.	

(*b*)

Fortunately,	production is now back to normal. work has now resumed. the staff have now gone back to work.

Write two sentences from *(a)* and *(b)*.

If you want to hide the real reason for the problem (your boss has been sitting on the order for three weeks, you have lost the order, thrown it away by mistake, or filed it in the wrong place), you can write

it was	caused by due to	an oversight on our part circumstances beyond our control

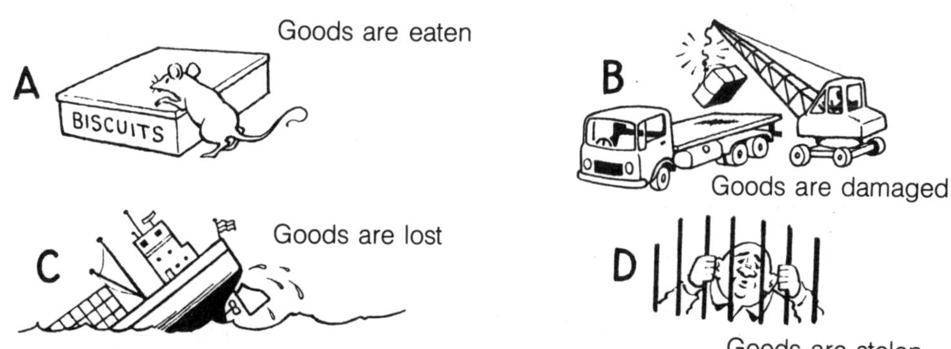

Circumstances beyond our control

2 *A mistake in the order* (This can also be used for a *delay* if there is not a good reason.)

We have	looked into investigated	your complaint the matter	and found that it was	caused by due to	a computer error an error oversight	in our	packing dispatch forwarding sales export	department.

Write two sentences.

C *What you propose to do*

The right goods Boots of the correct size The correct number of pans The replacement articles The 'Falcon 25' typewriters	have now been	forwarded dispatched	to you and you should receive them by	next week. 23rd March. the end of this month.

With regard to Regarding	the	wrong size goods incorrect articles defective machines wrong colour paint unwanted articles	you can return them to us. If you decide to keep	them it	we will offer you a	10% 20% 50%	discount on our list price.

Write two sentences

D *Apologise*

<table>
<tr><td rowspan="3">We apologise
for any inconvenience
caused by this</td><td rowspan="3">delay
error
oversight</td><td rowspan="3">and hope that</td><td colspan="3">it will not happen again.</td></tr>
<tr><td>you will</td><td>accept
agree to</td><td>our proposals.</td></tr>
<tr><td colspan="3">these arrangements will meet with your approval</td></tr>
</table>

Write two sentences

a letter from Mars

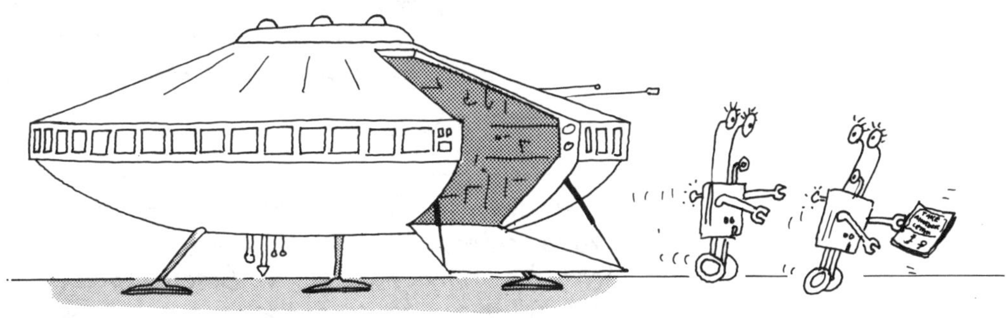

These are all the longest words from the 'Building up the letter' section (in Martian, of course!) In English they all begin with a vowel (= a, e, i, o, u). What are they?

1 PAPLOVAR = approval
2 RUSTINDILA =
3 URETBOKA =
4 NEDANTWU =
5 GALPOOSIE =
6 GORTHIVES =
7 MARNETSARGEN =
8 DASEGTINIVET =
9 ENNIOCVEENNCI =
10 YLLANOITPECXE =

3 Now write a reply to Miss Papas's letter about the wrong number of Kitchen King copper pans.

Look at this conversation to help you.

Ten minutes later . . .

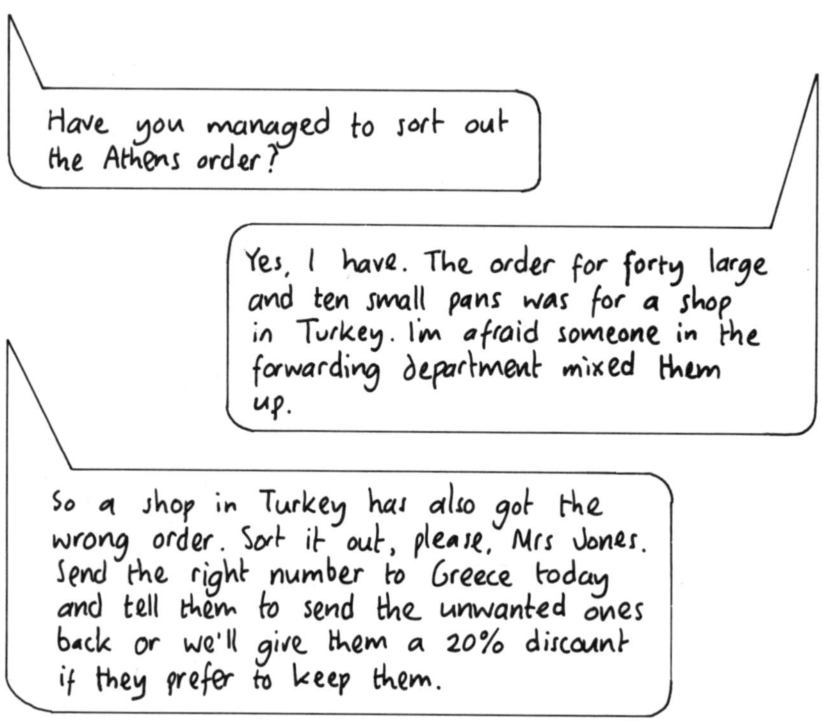

4 Prepositions

NOTE

ON time = punctually, at the right time.
IN time = not too late.

Example: The bus arrived ON time at 8.10, but we were not IN time for the beginning of the film, which began at 8.00.

BY = before, at the latest.

Example: We must receive the goods BY the end of the month.

Now fill in the blanks with the correct preposition.

1 They made a mistake ____ our order. What was the reason ____ this?
2 They sent us three size 4 instead ____ size 5.
3 You can now buy these books ____ a reduced price.
4 Could we have a computer ____ trial?
5 These circumstances were ____ our control. We will send replacements ____ air.
6 Return the faulty machines ____ our expense.
7 The consignment arrived on 30 November as planned. It was ____ time. It was also ____ time to go ____ sale ____ Christmas.
8 This delay ____ delivery was due ____ an oversight.
9 We must receive this order ____ 30 June at the latest.
10 The secretary is ____ the phone.
'Yes, we have the A50 staplers ____ stock. The B100 heavy-duty stapler?
No, I'm afraid we're ____ ____ stock of those.'
11 I'm sure they didn't pack the glasses incorrectly ____ purpose, so they must have done it ____ mistake.

5 Vocabulary exercise

Find the word meaning the same as the ones underlined. They are all new in this unit.

1 The factory has started production again. ________
2 We are sorry for this inconvenience. ________
3 This mistake was caused by the computer. ________
4 With regard to your letter of 10 July . . . ________
5 Please send back the defective parts. ________
6 These things that happened were beyond my control. ________
7 We have looked into your complaint. ________
8 We did not see the second page of your order.
This was a bad mistake on our part. ________

6 Vocabulary exercise

OPPOSITES

Opposites are usually formed by adding *in*, *un* or *dis* at the beginning. Example: correct, *in*correct; wanted, *un*wanted; advantage, *dis*advantage.

Look at these.

in	convenience correct (ly)	un	attractive competitive fortunate (ly) wanted	dis	advantage agree approval satisfied

Now use each of these ten opposites once in this conversation.

Whizzo-Kola

The drink that went flop, not pop!

The story so far. Last year the new 'Whizzo-Kola' was introduced. Sales dropped immediately. Now the president, Sir Billy Bubble, wants to know just why. He's talking to his sales manager, Mr Fred Froth.

Why isn't Whizzo-Kola selling well, Mr Froth?

Well, Sir Billy, there are three big ______________. The first is the price. At £2 a bottle it is simply ______________. And second, the new bottle. The customers think it is very ______________.

I ___________ with you, Froth. I personally find the new bottle very attractive. Don't forget, my wife, Lady Bubble, designed it herself! It looks like her.

Maybe, Sir, but the customers don't like it at all. In fact, it only meets with ______________. And the third problem is the taste, Sir. The customers don't like it. They say it tastes like medicine. They are very ______________ with it. And there are millions of ___________ bottles in our warehouse now, and this is causing us very great ______________, because we haven't got any room left to store anything else.

But someone told me that sales were up 10,000 this month.

I'm afraid that figure is ______________, Sir. The truth is we haven't sold one single bottle this month.

Oh dear! Not one? How ______________!

7 Verbs and Prepositions

Here is another exercise on verbs and prepositions (or adverb particles). Fill in the blanks with words from the list. Some of them are used several times.

BACK FOR INTO OFF OUT TO UP WITH

1 Thank him _____ his letter and say we are sorry _____ this oversight and that we hope the problem has now been sorted _____.
2 There is a wonderful offer in this advertisement. I'll write _____ now.
3 We have looked _____ the matter and found that our forwarding department mixed _____ the orders. We apologise _____ this error. If you don't want the wrong goods, you can send them _____.
4 They have replied _____ my counter-proposal, but they didn't agree _____ my suggestion.
5 There's the new 'Orange' personal computer. Let's go into the shop and try it _____.
6 'Oh dear! I forgot to send _____ that letter.' 'In that case, why don't you ring them _____. It'll be quicker.'
7 The taste of the new drink was so bad it didnt meet _____ anyone's approval.

8 Did you know

that the world's shortest exchange of letters was in 1862. The French writer Victor Hugo (1802–1885) was on holiday and wanted to find out from his publishers about the sales of his new novel, *Les Misérables*. He bought a postcard and wrote

The publishers replied

9 Dictation

In this dictation the secretary is talking to a new junior clerk.

Back up task

1 Look at the letters you wrote on p.64

Now write the reply. The boss is telling the secretary what to write.

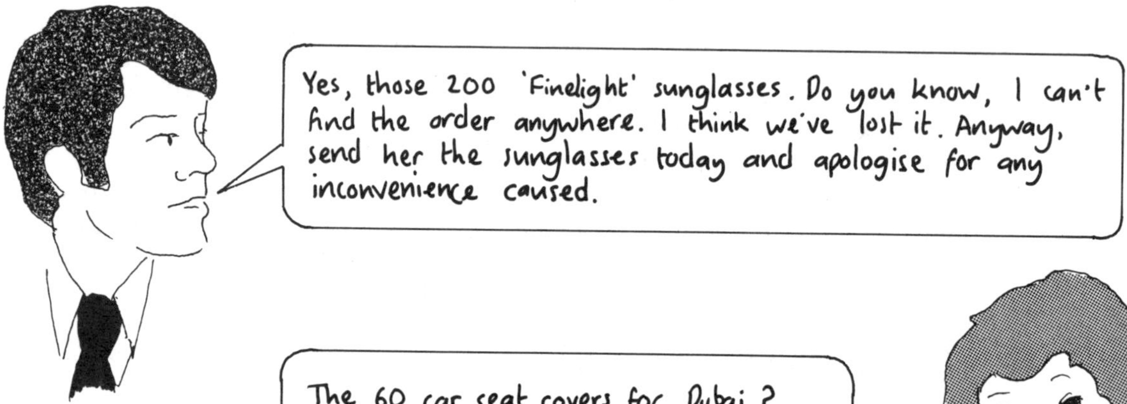

2 Now listen and take notes. Then reply to the letters you wrote on p.64.

A

B

Unit 8

Payments and reminders

1 In international trade there are different methods of payment. Very large sums are paid by Letter of Credit, a system of payment arranged through the buyer's and the seller's banks.

Smaller amounts can be paid by International Money Order. In this case you order the goods and receive a Pro Forma Invoice from the seller, which tells you how much to pay, often including all the insurance and transport costs. You can pay the invoice at your bank, then send the IMO to the seller, who will then send you the goods. Or, of course, you can ask the bank to transfer the money to his account, if you know the number. In some countries you can also pay by International Postal Order at the post office.

When companies do business regularly and trust each other, the buyer usually has an account with the seller. In this case he doesn't always pay each bill as it comes. The seller sends him a *monthly* or *quarterly* statement, listing all the bills to be paid. In modern business, to save time, when you make payment you simply send your cheque with the *Remittance Advice*, which is part of the invoice or statement. No covering letter is necessary.

Due = payable

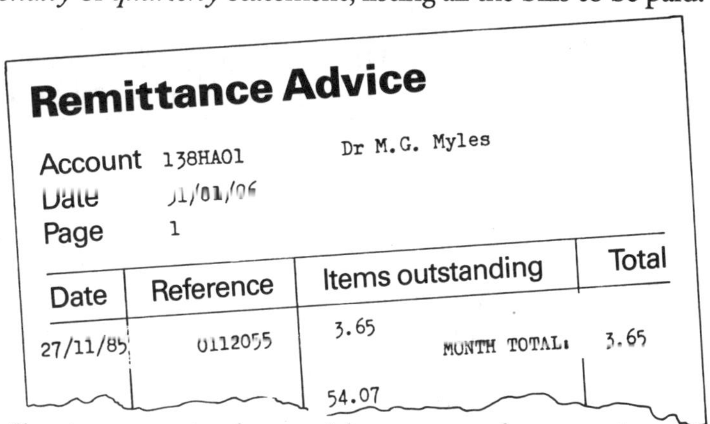

Remittance Advice

Account 138HA01   Dr M.G. Myles

Date 31/01/86

Page 1

Date	Reference	Items outstanding	Total
27/11/85	0112055	3.65 MONTH TOTAL:	3.65
		54.07	

However, some people still write a covering letter with payments, for example:

Dear Sirs

<u>Account No. H4002-26</u>

We have just received our quarterly statement for January - March.

Please find enclosed a cheque for £152 in settlement.

Yours faithfully

2 But payment is sometimes a problem!

The First Reminder

A Building up the letter
You refer to the invoice, statement or account and sometimes enclose a copy of it.

We refer to	your quarterly statement to 30 June your monthly statement for April the enclosed statement for September our invoice No. A 39429 for £28	and would like

to remind you that	the balance of £372 the sum of £450 this	is now overdue.

Write two sentences.

____

____

____

____

B Ask for payment

We are sure that	this is due to an oversight you have overlooked this	and would ask you	to settle the account invoice to send your remittance cheque	as soon as possible. without delay.

Write two sentences.

3 Write Mrs Barker's letter. Mr Howard's account is No. 4904-X.

4 If this reminder doesn't bring the payment, then what?

The Second Reminder

It is usual to send a second reminder if the first one has no effect.

Most large companies today don't send a second reminder – it costs money and wastes time. They send a *final notice* immediately.

However, smaller companies, for whom every customer is important, might still send a second reminder.

Building up the letter

A

In our letter of ____ we	pointed out reminded you	that	payment settlement of	your quarterly statement to 31 March our invoice No. A 39429	was overdue. was outstanding.

Write one sentence.

____

____

B

You will	understand realise	that we also have our obligations and we therefore

look forward to receiving hope you will send us	your	remittance payment cheque settlement	without delay. by return. by 30 June. within seven days.

Write two sentences.

____

____

____

____

____

____

5 Now write Mrs Barker's second reminder, using different sentences from the ones you have just written.

6 And if you still don't get your money? There's usually a good reason.

Has Mr Howard paid that outstanding account yet? It's now nearly three months overdue.

No, I'm afraid he hasn't replied to either of our letters, of 3rd March and 4th April.

I wonder why he's so late this time?

Well, you know, ever since they opened the new road three months ago, cars don't drive through the town any more.

And a good thing that is too, Mrs Barker. It's much cleaner and quieter now.

Yes, but that means that cars don't stop and fill up with petrol at Howard's Garage any more. His business has been badly hit and he's probably got debts.

Yes, perhaps he's in debt now. In that case, why didn't he write and explain about his inability to pay? Well, we can't wait any longer now.

Shall I send him a final notice?

Yes. Tell him to pay within one week. And say that if he doesn't, we'll have to place the matter in the hands of our solicitors.

The Final Notice

If your first two reminders are unsuccessful you will have to write a third, and last one. This is called the *final notice* and it is different, because now you say that you will have to take legal steps to recover your money. This usually has an effect!

Normally a final notice is sent by registered post, so that the addressee cannot say that he never received it.

Building up the letter

A Refer to the two unanswered reminders.

We have had no reply to our letters of _____ and _____	in which we pointed out reminded you pointing out reminding you	that the sum of _____ is now overdue.

Write one sentence.

____

____

B You threaten legal action.

We regret to inform you that if	settlement	is not received	within seven days
	payment		by 31 March

the matter will be placed		in the hands of our solicitors.
we shall be obliged to	place the matter	lawyers.
	take legal steps.	
	action.	

Write two sentences.

____

____

____

____

____

____

7 Now write Mrs Barker's final notice.

8 Dictation

9 Vocabulary exercise

New words: debtor = the person who owes money. He has *debts* to pay.
creditor = the person to whom money is owed.

Who likes paying bills?

1 The debtor's point of view.
Fill in the blanks. All the words begin with 'o'.

Who likes paying bills? Probably no ____. I certainly don't! I know I should really pay them __ time, because the person I ___ money to, the creditor, has also got his ______________. But I usually pay my bills late. They're all months _____ ___ by the time I finally pay them. __ course, when I get a final notice I pay and apologise, saying that I have simply '_______ _____ their invoice', in ______ words, I 'forgot' to pay, or sometimes I say that it was 'due to an ___________'.
I sometimes have dozens of bills __________ ___. Why do I do this? Because I can leave the money in my bank and they pay me interest!

2 The creditor's point of view.
Fill in the blanks using the words given in the box.

account	inconvenience
action	interest
amount	recover
arrears	reminder
cash	settle
debt	solicitor
effect	statement
fees	threaten
final notice	waste

It's all right for you. As a shopkeeper you can simply say, 'if you don't pay ______ now, you won't get the goods'. But it's very annoying for me, as your creditor, if customers like you are in ______ with large ______ of money because they haven't ______ their ______, although they have received their regular monthly or quarterly ______. Then I have to write a first and second ______, and that costs money and ______ my secretary's time. And if that doesn't have any ______, I have the trouble of sending a ______ ______ and I even have to ______ my customer with legal ______. In other words, I may have to ask a ______ to ______ my money for me. Then, of course, someone has to pay the solicitor's ______. He doesn't work for nothing! If I am not careful, I will be the one who is in ______! So the whole business causes a lot of unnecessary expense and ______, to say nothing of the fact that, while I am waiting, I have to borrow money from the bank and pay them.

10 Vocabulary exercise

Fill in the correct form of the word given. The endings (suffixes) are

-ABLE -AL -ANCE -URE

1 I'm afraid this (PROPOSE) ______ doesn't meet with the boss's (APPROVE) ______ at all.
2 This particular model is not (AVAIL) ______ at the moment.
3 They want to have the machine on (TRY) ______ to see if it gives a good (PERFORM) ______.
4 If you have any (ENCLOSE) ______, don't forget to put them into the envelope with the letter! And don't forget the (SIGN) ______.
5 Our terms are: half with order, half on (ACCEPT) ______ of the goods.
6 If you hire your car through us, we will arrange the (INSURE) ______ and have it ready for your (ARRIVE) ______ at the airport. We will also collect it on your (DEPART) ______.
7 Goods like fruit and vegetables are (PERISH) ______. They must be delivered quickly.
8 The World Bank spends a lot of money on (AGRICULTURE) ______ and (EDUCATION) ______ projects all over the world.
9 You must be careful when you transport glass, which is (BREAK) ______, and liquids like petrol, which are (INFLAME) ______.
10 With many car (RENT) ______ firms you have to pay a (RETURN) ______ deposit. And you have to pay extra for (CONTINENT) ______ hire.

Back up task

1 Here is a computer print-out of some outstanding monthly accounts.

Write reminders for one or two which are only a little overdue and final notices for the ones which are very late.

MONTHLY STATEMENTS OVERDUE AS AT: 15 06 198.

DATE DUE	SUM OUTSTANDING	ACCOUNT NO.	ACCOUNT HOLDER
31 03	$3700.00	B-1429	Hobson & Co
31 03	$ 256.70	B-1290	Laird & Biffin
30 04	$ 728.50	A-625	Tyler Inc
30 04	$ 14.00	B-1302	Mr C. Davies
31 05	$2942.00	C-728	Wills & Frost
31 05	$ 182.50	A-1927	Mrs J. Broughton

2 Now reply to one of these reminders, enclosing your cheque in settlement. Also apologise for the delay in payment and any inconvenience caused.

Little words out of big words

SECRETARY
How many smaller words can you find in this word?
Each letter can be used once only in your word. There are a lot of small words in this one, so if you find 15 words, good. 25 words, very good. 40 words, excellent!

Do it together in class. There are certainly more than 50 words, not counting plurals and third person singular (eg eat/eats).

Unit 9

Applying for a job

1 Look carefully at the advertisements below and then listen to the cassette. Decide which job is being discussed.

The abbreviations are all listed on p. 90.

SECRETARIAL

Managing Director

of a well-known art publisher requires a competent, enthusiastic

SECRETARY/P.A.

to help in the smooth running of the office. A well educated, experienced person is needed, preferably over the age of twenty-five. Must have administrative ability and good secretarial skills to include WP and PC work. Good English essential, foreign language an advantage.

Excellent salary, negotiable.

For further information and application form, telephone

01-731 2900

EDITORIAL SECRETARY

SUNDAY COLOUR SUPPLEMENT

requires an enthusiastic Editorial Secretary to work for the picture desk and art desk. Good shorthand and typing is required and a competent telephone manner. Age 19 years plus.

Hectic department, liaising with Photographers and Picture Agencies. Picture Desk experience would be an advantage. Hours 10 - 5 30, 6 weeks holiday. Offices close to Blackfriars Station.

Salary £159.43 per week.

For more information please ring
01-353 6000 extension 525

Work in advertising

SEC/PA to Chief Executive required by leading advertising agency.
Well educated, friendly person 25-45.
Good secretarial and organisational skills. Wpm 70/SH 100, WP experience. Must have minimum GCE 'O' level English and preferably French/German.
Interest in colour/design advantage.
40-hr week, LVs, generous holidays.
Salary negotiable, min. £10,000.

Send CV and covering letter to

L & V Whattam Ltd
124 St. Anne Street
London
WC1 3AB

TYNE TEES TELE

have a vaca

SECRE

LONDON

Salary £8,90

Tyne Tees Enterprises, o
Sales Department selling
world, now have the opp
excellent secretarial skills
television, to join the te
Ideally you will have th
people at all levels; be
and participate in the
department and both de
on your own initiative a
A flexible approach is e
particularly in French,
We offer an attractive
season ticket loan, lu
scheme.
If you think you could
demanding please wr
application form and
Personnel Manager,
City Road, Newcastl
Tyne Tees gives full
applicants irrespecti

AUDIO TYPIST

PUBLISHING

£7,500-£8,250

Sales Department seeks person to assist Export Sales Manager. The work will involve audio typing, general office management etc. Some office experience helpful.

Ring:
01-636 4622 ext 600

SECRETARY/ ASSISTANT

This is an excellent opportunity to join the fast-moving and exciting world of book publishing, with one of Britain's leading publishing houses, based in Mayfair.
Working primarily for the Marketing Director, you will be involved in all departmental activities, assisting his busy team.
Fast, accurate typing, sound organisational ability and at least six months secretarial experience are required for this very varied and demanding position.
We offer plenty of challenge, a salary of £7,000–£7,500 plus a number of attractive benefits.
To apply please phone 01-493 7070 or write, enclosing a full C.V. to: **Melanie Laing, Personnel Officer, COLLINS PUBLISHERS, 8 Grafton Street, London W1X 3LA.**

GRAFTON BOOKS

A Division of the Collins Publishing Group.

GRADUA

The Marketing Mana
years experience to
RISL, a well establ
supplier of softwar
The job requires
disposition.
For this appointm
Thames, fluency i
French Parent Co
as would knowled
In exchange we
contributory pensi
Please

RAND IN
29 Thames

COUNTRY ESTATES

They'll keep you busy in St. James's helping to administer farms and parkland.

Lovely offices, variety, happy atmosphere.

Your natural confidence, ability with people and competent shorthand/typing will all be needed in this very special job. C. £8,700 + free lunch, free

SECRETARIES

We are looking for two bright, enthusiastic and well educated secretaries, with good shorthand and typing skills to work for the Associates and their teams in our busy, friendly Architectural Practice.

Salary within range £6,000-

SECRETARY — £8,000

For young friendly company in West End. Great opportunity for lively presentable young person. WP/shorthand, interested in marketing. Salary review after six months.

Contact Lindy on:

01-404 5620/831 6555

INTERNATI DESIGN O

seeks experienced s
partner. As well as
typist and organiser
intelligent, liter
methodical, accura
humorous, patient,
hard-working and

Write to: Barbar

2 Now listen to the conversation again and answer the questions. Stop the cassette where necessary.

1 What are the two men called? ____________________

2 What is their present secretary called? ____________________

3 When will she be leaving? ____________________

4 What don't they want to do after she leaves?

____

____

5 What sort of person does the manager NOT want?

____

6 What sort of person DOES he want?

____

____

7 What special qualities must the applicant have?

p__________ and i__________.

8 Is organisational ability more important than typing for this job?

____

9 Why do they need someone with French or German?

____

____

10 What is their present secretary's salary? ____________________

11 What does the manager first suggest the new PA's salary should be?

____

12 Does it say how many weeks holiday they give?

____

What will the new secretary's name be? ____________________

To find out, take the first letter of the missing word.

She must be able to
She mustn't sit there filing her
Her salary is
She must be young and

3 Writing a *curriculum vitae.*

When you apply for a job, most large companies send you their own application form to fill in (see next page). But for a job in a small firm, you usually have to make up your own curriculum vitae.

This is the one Anne Price wrote to send to L & V Whattam.

Curriculum Vitae

Anne L. Price

Personal Details

Address: 90 Mortimer Court
11 Abbey Road
London NW8

Date of birth: 6/2/59
Place of birth: Edinburgh
Marital Status: single

Tel: 01-289 5274

Education

Leith Road Primary School 1965-70
Sir Walter Scott High School 1970-76
Westend Secretarial College, London 1978-79

"Introduction to Computers" evening course
North London Polytechnic 1982-83

Exams

GCE 'O' Level English Language, French, Maths, History, Art

Secretarial Experience

Various temporary jobs (to gain experience) 1979
James & Walker, Estate Agents 1980-83
Erskine Fraser, Solicitors 1983-

Other Experience

Worked as au-pair girl in France 1976-78

Two tips about writing a CV.

1) Always put down anything interesting, or special, you have done, all courses etc. They might not seem important to you, but your future employer might think they are useful (eg, Anne Price writes that she has worked as an au-pair girl in France. This means that her spoken French is probably quite good. It tells her employer more about her French than GCE 'O' Level French!)

2) Make sure every year is mentioned. Any year where you do not write down what you were doing will make the employer ask questions!

4 Now write your own CV.

5 Listen to the conversation and fill in the application form for this candidate.

Laurie Alexander

AFFIX PHOTO HERE

APPLICATION FOR EMPLOYMENT
CONFIDENTIAL
Fill in IN BLOCK LETTERS

Position applied for ____________________

Personal details

Full name ____________________

Address ____________________

____

Tel ____________________

Date of birth __________ Place of birth __________

Nationality __________ Driving licence __________

Education (give dates)

Secondary ____________________

Further ____________________

____

Exams/diplomas obtained ____________________

Previous employment (give dates)

____

____

Other experience (give details of any special personal interests which you think may be relevant to your application)

____

____

References

Please give names of two referees (NOT a member of your family)

Professional ____________________

____

Personal ____________________

____

Date __________ Signature __________

6 Now fill in an application form for yourself.

Laurie Alexander

AFFIX PHOTO HERE

APPLICATION FOR EMPLOYMENT
CONFIDENTIAL
Fill in IN BLOCK LETTERS

Position applied for ____________________

Personal details

Full name ____________________

Address ____________________

____

Tel ____________________

Date of birth ____________ Place of birth ____________

Nationality ____________ Driving licence ____________

Education (give dates)

Secondary ____________________

Further ____________________

____

Exams/diplomas obtained ____________________

Previous employment (give dates)

____

____

Other experience (give details of any special personal interests which you think may be relevant to your application)

____

____

References

Please give names of two referees (NOT a member of your family)

Professional ____________________

____

Personal ____________________

____

Date ____________ Signature ____________

7 The covering letter.

The covering letter, quite often handwritten, should:

1 refer to the advertisement
2 give a brief summary of your experience, referring especially to experience which will be useful in the new job
3 say why you are leaving your old job / why the new job attracts you.

Look at the letter which Anne Price wrote.

90 Mortimer Court
11 Abbey Road
London NW8 4AY

Tel 01-289 5274

L & V Whattam Ltd
124 St Anne Street
London WC1 3AB

Dear Sirs

I have seen your advertisment in today's "Daily News" and I would like to apply for the post of Personal Assistant.

As you can see from the enclosed curriculum vitae, I have had several years' experience in different offices. In both my last jobs the organisational side was very important and there was a lot of work using the computer.

However, I would now prefer a post where I can use my knowledge of French and where my interest in art might be useful.

I hope you will consider my application and look forward to hearing from you.

Yours faithfully

Anne L. Price

Anne L. Price

Enc. Curriculum Vitae

8 Building up the letter

These letters are all very personal, so it is possible only to give general guidelines. This section develops the three important points of the covering letter.

A Refer to the advertisement
If there are several posts advertised you must say which one you are applying for.

With reference to I have seen	your advertisement in the '......'	and	I would like to apply I am interested in applying	for	this post the post of	Personal Assistant. Secretary to the Sales Manager

Write a sentence like this.

____

____

____

B Summarise your experience

As you can see from the enclosed CV I have had	long one year's many years'	experience in	different fields. banking / insurance / legal work etc the hotel business industry.	In my last jobs/positions In all my jobs In my present job

the administrative organisational secretarial artistic public relations financial	side aspect	was is	extremely very	important and I	worked a lot with computers. ran the office independently. learnt to work under pressure. managed the bookkeeping.

Write two sentences.

____

____

____

____

____

____

____

____

____

C Why the new job interests you

However, although	I like I am happy in I am satisfied with	my present job, position,	I would now prefer a post I am now looking for a post	offering more responsibility. more chances of promotion.	
				where I can use my	administrative skills. knowledge of languages. financial knowledge. legal knowledge.

Write two sentences

9 Now look at the advertisements again and choose a job. Write the covering letter that you would send with your CV.

SECRETARIAL

Managing Director

of a well-known art publisher requires a competent, enthusiastic

SECRETARY/P.A.

to help in the smooth running of the office. A well educated, experienced person is needed, preferably over the age of twenty-five. Must have administrative ability and good secretarial skills to include WP and PC work. Good English essential, foreign language an advantage.

Excellent salary, negotiable.

For further information and application form, telephone

01-731 2900

EDITORIAL SECRETARY

SUNDAY COLOUR SUPPLEMENT

requires an enthusiastic Editorial Secretary to work for the picture desk and art desk. Good shorthand and typing is required and a competent telephone manner. Age 19 years plus.

Hectic department, liaising with Photographers and Picture Agencies. Picture Desk experience would be an advantage. Hours 10 - 5 30, 6 weeks holiday. Offices close to Blackfriars Station.

Salary £159.43 per week.

For more information please ring 01-353 6000 extension 525

TYNE TEES TELEVISION

have a vacancy for a

SECRET

LONDON OF

Salary £8,900 per

Tyne Tees Enterprises, our success
Sales Department selling programn
world, now have the opportunity fo
excellent secretarial skills (100/50),
television, to join the team.
Ideally you will have the confider
people at all levels; be self motiva
and participate in the day-to-day o
department and both demonstrate the
on your own initiative and as part of a
A flexible approach is essential, and lingu
particularly in French, are highly desira
We offer an attractive benefits package
season ticket loan, lunch allowance an
scheme.
If you think you could meet the level of
demanding please write, enclosing an
application form and job description to
Personnel Manager, Tyne Tees Televis
City Road, Newcastle upon Tyne NE1 2
Tyne Tees gives full and fair considera
applicants irrespective of sex, marital sta

Work in advertising

SEC/PA to Chief Executive required by leading advertising agency.
Well educated, friendly person 25-45.
Good secretarial and organisational skills. Wpm 70/SH 100. WP experience. Must have minimum GCE 'O' level English and preferably French/German.
Interest in colour/design advantage.
40-hr week, LVs, generous holidays.
Salary negotiable, min. £10,000.

Send CV and covering letter to

L & V Whattam Ltd
124 St. Anne Street
London
WC1 3AB

AUDIO TYPIST

PUBLISHING

£7,500-£8,250

Sales Department seeks person to assist Export Sales Manager. The work will involve audio typing, general office management etc. Some office experience helpful.

Ring:
01-636 4622 ext 600

SECRETARY/ ASSISTANT

This is an excellent opportunity to join the fast-moving and exciting world of book publishing, with one of Britain's leading publishing houses, based in Mayfair.
Working primarily for the Marketing Director, you will be involved in all departmental activities, assisting his busy team.
Fast, accurate typing, sound organisational ability and at least six months secretarial experience are required for this very varied and demanding position.
We offer plenty of challenge, a salary of £7,000–£7,500 plus a number of attractive benefits.
To apply please phone 01-493 7070 or write, enclosing a full C.V. to: **Melanie Laing, Personnel Officer, COLLINS PUBLISHERS, 8 Grafton Street, London W1X 3LA.**

GRAFTON BOOKS
A Division of the Collins Publishing Group.

GRADUATE SECRET

The Marketing Manager needs a Secretary, with
years experience to assist him and his team t
RISL, a well established hi-tech company, int
supplier of software services to clients in Eur
The job requires a dynamic person with
disposition.
For this appointment, which is based in Kin
Thames, fluency in French for communicat
French Parent Company would be a disting
as would knowledge of word-processors.
In exchange we offer: Salary circa £9,500
contributory pension, very pleasant modern

Please apply in writing with CV t
Sara Wilkinson,
RAND INFORMATION SYSTEMS
29 Thames Street, Kingston-upon-T
Surrey KT1 1PS.
Non-smoking environment

COUNTRY ESTATES

They'll keep you busy in St. James's helping to administer farms and parkland.

Lovely offices, variety, happy atmosphere.

Your natural confidence, ability with people and competent shorthand/typing will all be needed in this very special job. C. £8,700 + free lunch, free parking, etc.

01-370 5066

Hendersons

SECRETARIES

We are looking for two bright, enthusiastic and well educated secretaries, with good shorthand and typing skills to work for the Associates and their teams in our busy, friendly Architectural Practice.

Salary within range £6,000-£8,500 aae.

Please write or phone Carol Aylett, Pollard Thomas & Edwards, 55 Colebrook Row, London N1 8AF, Tel

SECRETARY — £8,000

For young friendly company in West End. Great opportunity for lively presentable young person. WP/shorthand, interested in marketing. Salary review after six months.

Contact Lindy on:

01-404 5620/831 6555

INTERNATIONAL DESIGN OFFICE

seeks experienced secretary for partner. As well as an excellent typist and organiser she must be intelligent, literate, neat, methodical, accurate, dedicated, humorous, patient, persevering, hard-working and presentable.

Write to: Barbara Brown, 11 Needham Road, London W11 2RP, enclosing c.v. and handwritten letter.

BOOSEY & HAWKES MUSIC PUBLISHERS

require a

10 Vocabulary exercise

Sir V. Rich requires a new personal assistant. Fill in the blanks with words from the box.

administrative competent efficient enthusiastic essential experience independently initiative negotiable pressure promotion responsibility run skills

Wondergirl Secretarial Agency. Can I help you?

Good morning. Sir Vernon Rich speaking. I need a new PA.

Yes, Sir Vernon. What sort of person are you looking for?

Well, someone who can do the job well, someone who is very __________ and __________, and who is keen, you know, __________. In this job organisational and ability is more important than secretarial __________.

And I suppose you want someone who can work under __________.

Yes, and she must be able to work on her own __________ and be able to __________ the office __________, especially when I'm not here, which is most of the time. All those business lunches, and golf, you know. Yes, this is a position of great

And the salary?

Not very large, I'm afraid, but it'll be depending on age and __________.

And I suppose you want someone very beautiful?

Of course, most important, __________, in fact.

Are there any chances of __________?

No, not in the job itself. But if she's got all these qualities and can cook well too, then I might ask her to become Lady Rich.

In that case, I think I've found just the right person.

Who?

ME!!

Revision

The case of the CRAZY KITCHEN

A Complete Exchange of Correspondence

Step 1: *Finding the market*

You are the PA to the boss of EASIMATIC 'do-it-yourself' kitchens, which are now selling well in your country. Your boss (find a name for him) is going to exhibit some kitchens at the Ideal Home Exhibition in London because he wants to get into the British market. He is going over to London to help arrange the exhibition and to arrange an advertising campaign and look for agents and stockists. Write all the relevant letters and their replies.

Now, here are the details of my London trip. Arrival at Heathrow 11.30 on March 22nd, departure from Heathrow, 17.30 on March 27nd. Please arrange a meeting with L + V Whattam to discuss our advertising campaign.

Mr Whattam replies, suggesting a date.

I also want you to hire a car for me for the whole period. Get me a Jaguar or a Porsche. I like sports cars. Write to Wiley's Car Rental.

Wiley's (their address is on p. 15) send a quotation (look at table on p. 18).

And don't forget to fix my hotel accommodation in London for the nights of 22nd, 23rd and 26th March. Single room. Try one of the luxury hotels, the Hilton or the Dorchester.

Confirm hotel booking. Give prices.

Step 2: ***The sales figures rise***

Ray Harris is a stockist of kitchens in Woolhampton, a town in the English Midlands. He has seen the EASIMATIC do-it-yourself kitchens at the exhibition in London and got their brochures and price list. He would like to stock them but as he drives home he is already thinking what he will tell his secretary to write the next morning.

Write a letter.

A week later.

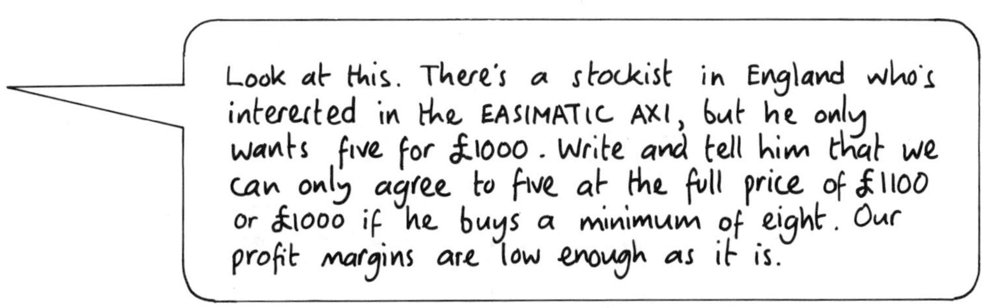

Step 3: *Things go wrong*

Six months later. Mr Ray Harris of Woolhampton has sold the kitchens and has ordered some more. Everything is going well, until a Dr D. Miles comes into the shop. He orders an EASIMATIC AX1 and pays one third (£600) as a deposit. When the consignment of kitchens arrives there are problems with Dr Miles's light green one.

1 The consignment arrives very late.
2 One whole unit is badly damaged and unusable.
3 Three drawers are broken.
4 The sink unit is not the same colour as the others.

Mr Harris writes demanding an explanation and immediate replacement, to be sent direct to Dr Miles.

There's a letter of complaint from Mr Harris about the AX1 light green kitchen we sent. First, apologise for the delay. That was due to the strike we had in the factory. And send the replacements immediately, direct to Dr Miles.

But we don't make the AX1 any more. We'll have to send parts from the BX2.

OK, but write to Mr Harris now.

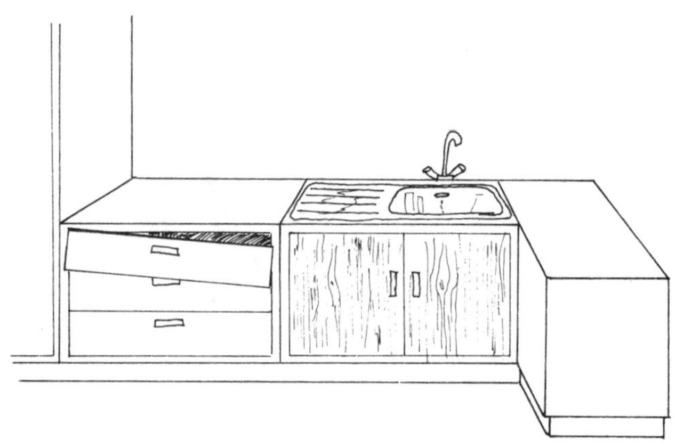

Three weeks later.

Dr Miles receives the kitchen but finds that the colour of the new BX2 replacement is not the same as the AX1, and the new drawers don't fit. He writes direct to the company saying that they must now supply a complete new BX2 kitchen at the same price as the AX1, and they can take the old AX1 units away at their expense.

He says to his wife.

Thank goodness I only paid one third of the kitchen.

That's quite enough! We've only got one third of the kitchen so far!

In the meantime in Woolhampton.

Dr Miles has only paid one third deposit. He's got his kitchen now, so the rest is overdue. Write him a reminder. The sale price of the AX1 is £1800 so he owes us £1200.

One month later.

Dr Miles still hasn't paid for the kitchen. Send him a final notice. He must pay within two weeks.

In Dr Miles's house.

Mr Harris can put the matter in the hands of his solicitors if he wants to. I'm still waiting for my BX2 kitchen, and if it doesn't arrive within one month I'm going to put the matter in the hands of MY solicitors. I'm going to write a blockbuster to the manager of EASIMATIC and tell him what I think!

Step 4: *Rats leave the sinking ship*

Meanwhile at EASIMATIC headquarters business is going very badly. Your competitors have a better kitchen and are taking your market away. Your boss is still paying the workers badly and there has been another strike. There is talk of a takeover by the rival firm. You are now sitting with a blockbuster from a Dr Miles in England and you feel that the time has come for a change of job. Reading through the paper you see this super job. Apply for it – and GOOD LUCK!

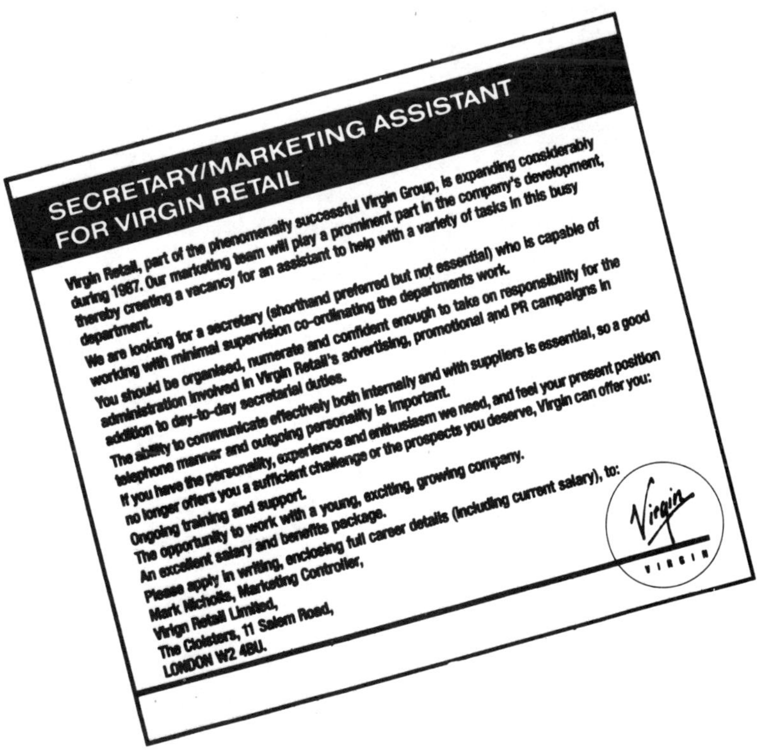

SECRETARY/MARKETING ASSISTANT FOR VIRGIN RETAIL

Virgin Retail, part of the phenomenally successful Virgin Group, is expanding considerably during 1987. Our marketing team will play a prominent part in the company's development, thereby creating a vacancy for an assistant to help with a variety of tasks in this busy department.

We are looking for a secretary (shorthand preferred but not essential) who is capable of working with minimal supervision co-ordinating the departments work.

You should be organised, numerate and confident enough to take on responsibility for the administration involved in Virgin Retail's advertising, promotional and PR campaigns in addition to day-to-day secretarial duties.

The ability to communicate effectively both internally and with suppliers is essential, so a good telephone manner and outgoing personality is important.

If you have the personality, experience and enthusiasm we need, and feel your present position no longer offers you a sufficient challenge or the prospects you deserve, Virgin can offer you:

Ongoing training and support.

The opportunity to work with a young, exciting, growing company.

An excellent salary and benefits package.

Please apply in writing, enclosing full career details (including current salary), to:

Mark Nicholls, Marketing Controller,
Virgin Retail Limited,
The Cloisters, 11 Salem Road,
LONDON W2 4BU.

Abbreviations
used in this book

& and
% *per cent* (Latin) = in every hundred
$ dollar (money in US, Australia, New Zealand, Hong Kong etc.)
£ pound sterling (money in UK)
AA Automobile Association. Car club in UK. Helps if you have a breakdown
adj adjective
adv adverb
Bros brothers
CDW Collision Damage Waiver. If you hire a car in the UK you are fully covered by insurance except for the first £300 damage to the car if you have an accident. If you take out the CDW insurance, this sum is also covered.
CIF Cost, Insurance, Freight
Co. company
CV *curriculum vitae* (Latin) = short written summary of your education and experience.
CWO cash with order
e.g. *exempli gratia* (Latin) = for example
enc enclosure
esp especially
etc *et cetera* (Latin) = and the rest/and so on
GCE General Certificate of Education. British exam at the 'O' = ordinary level (taken at about age 15–17) and at the 'A' = advanced level (taken two years after 'O' level). Now replaced by GCSE (General Certificate of Secondary Education)
hr/hrs hour(s)
IBM International Business Machines. An American computer company
IMO International Money Order
Inc incorporated (US = corporation/large company)
L/C letter of credit
Ltd limited company
LV luncheon vouchers. Tickets given to employees so that they can have their midday meal at a restaurant.
min. minimum
n noun
neg. negotiable
No. number
p. page
PA personal assistant = a manager's secretary
PABX Private Automatic Branch Exchange, a switchboard
PC Personal computer
plc Private limited company
p.p. *per procurationem* (Latin) = for/on behalf of
prep preposition
Pty Proprietary (company)
RAC Royal Automobile Club. Car club in UK, like the AA.
ref reference
SH shorthand
tel telephone
tlx telex
UK United Kingdom (England, Wales, Scotland and Northern Ireland)
USA United States of America
v verb
VAT Value Added Tax
WP word processor
wpm words per minute (typing speed)

Business words
used in this book

account, *n* list or statement of money received and owing
acknowledge, *v* say that you have received something. **acknowledgement,** *n*
action, *n* industrial action: strike. Legal action: using the law
advertise, *v* tell people, make public announcement, e.g. in newspaper, on TV, to increase sales of goods etc. **advertising agent**: person who prepares/arranges your **advertisement,** *n*. **advertising campaign**: a lot of advertising (esp. to promote new goods or service)
agent, *n* person/company selling your goods, doing a service for you in his/their area or country
amount, *n* quantity
appointment, *n* (business) meeting
in arrears late with payment
assume, *v* believe, think (without actually knowing)
available, *adj* can be had, bought

balance, *n* the rest of an amount to be paid

cancel, *v* say that you no longer want something already ordered or reserved. **cancellation,** *n*
circumstances, *n* (usually plural) things that happen which you cannot control
compete, *v* **competitive,** *n*, **competition,** *n*, **competitor,** *n*: see p. 72 section 7
confirm, *v* say you will certainly do something, e.g. book a room. **confirmation,** *n*
consignment, *n* delivery of goods
to the contrary to the opposite
convenient, *adj* suitable (time and place). See also **inconvenience**
cover, *v, n* insure
creditor, *n* person to whom money is owed

deadline, *n* last date by which something must be done
debt, *n* money owed. **in debt**: owing money. **debtor,** *n* person who owes money
defective, *adj* not working correctly, partly broken
definite, *adj* certain, fixed
demonstrate, *v* show how something (esp. machine) works. **demonstration,** *n*
deposit, *n* a small amount of money you pay in advance (esp. on reservation) to show that you are a serious customer.
destination, *n* place you are going to or send goods to
discount, *n* amount or percentage taken off usual price
dispatch, *v, n* send
dispute, *n* disagreement (esp. between management and staff/workers)
document, *n* important paper giving information, e.g. driving licence, passport
due, *adj* payable. **due to**: caused by

enrol, *v* register for a course. **enrolment,** *n*
estimate, *n* offer to do a job at a certain price
executive, *n* important businessman
expire, *v* cease to be useable after a certain date, not be valid any more (e.g. passport, driving licence). **expiry,** *n*

faulty, *adj* same as **defective**
forward, *v* send, dispatch goods
fragile, *adj* can break easily
freight, *n* transport of goods by land, sea or air
further to, *prep* about, regarding

grant, *v* give/offer (a discount)

inconvenience, *n* difficulty or trouble (esp. when something goes wrong)
indicate, *v* show clearly. **indication,** *n*
inferior, *adj* poor (quality)
initial, *adj* first, at the beginning
insurance, *n* paying money to insure something (e.g. your car, your life) against loss or damage. **insurance cover**: being insured. **insurance proposal**: form you must fill in if you want insurance
interest, *n* percentage paid for borrowing money. e.g. the bank's interest rate is 10%
introduce, *v* bring in (a new product or service). **introductory offer**: cheaper price for new product to make it sell well at the beginning
investigate, *v* try to find out what has happened
item, *n* one of something, article in a list
itinerary, *n* detailed plan of a journey

line, *n* a type of goods

outstanding, *adj* not yet paid
overdue, *adj* late (esp. of payment)
overlook, *v* not to see something (by mistake)
oversight, *n* not seeing something (by mistake) (the noun of **overlook**)

perform, *v* work (of machines). **performance** *n*
premises, *n* (always plural) buildings, offices (esp. for business)
prepared to, *adj* ready to
produce, *v* make (goods). **producer,** *n* person/company making goods, **product,** *n* the goods made. **production,** *n* the action of making goods
promote, *v* advertise goods to make the public know about them. **promotion,** *n*

quarterly, *adj* every quarter, every three months
quote, *v* offer a price (for goods). **quotation,** *n*

range, *n* choice of goods
receipt, *n* noun from verb **receive. acknowledge receipt**
recover, *v* get (money) back
regret, *v* be sorry
remind, *v* tell someone they have forgotten (to pay). **reminder.** *n*
remittance, *n* payment (esp. sent in the post, e.g. cheque)
replace, *v* give one article instead of another (esp. a good one for a damaged one). **replacement,** *n*
representative, *n* salesman, agent
request, *v, n* ask for
require, *v* need. **requirement,** *n*
resume, *v* begin again (esp. work, after a break)
run, *v* organise, manage, e.g. a school, a hotel. **run low**: not have much stock left

scheme, *n* (official) plan or project
seconds, *n* (plural) poor quality article sold at a lower price
settle, *v* pay. **settlement,** *n*
slack, *adj* not busy
sold out have no more articles for sale. Note: The cakes *are* sold out, we *are* sold out of cakes.
solicitor, *n* lawyer (esp. in UK)
sort out, *v* put right, deal with (a problem)
statement, *n* list showing money paid/owed. **monthly statement. bank statement**
steps, *n* take legal steps: ask the law to help you
sterling, *n* British money, pounds sterling
stock, *v, n* offer goods for sale. **in stock/out of stock. stockist,** *n* person who stocks your goods regularly
strike, *v, n* not work (because of disagreement)
subject to, *prep* likely to, may possibly. Prices subject to change = can be changed at any time
submit, *v* give, offer (a quotation, estimate)
suggest, *v* say or write your idea, propose. **suggestion,** *n*
sum, *n* quantity of money

terms, *n* (plural) price, conditions of sale
therefore, *adj* so, for that reason
third-party (damage, injury) esp. in car insurance. In addition to the car and the driver the insurance company will also pay for any other thing you damage or person you injure
threaten, *v* warn
trial, *n* testing a product/machine to see if it sells/works well. trial order, trial period, have goods **on trial. Try out,** *v*
trust, *v* hope

urgently, *adv* (you need something) quickly, because it is important

warehouse, *n* place where you keep large quantities of goods